LIFE IN LOCKDOWN I:

THE GOOD, THE BAD & THE UGLY

Coping, resilience & positivity
– lessons from a worldwide pandemic

ALSO BY THE AUTHOR:

by I. S. Thorne

The Programme Trilogy:
The Programme
The Resistance

LIFE IN LOCKDOWN I:

THE GOOD, THE BAD & THE UGLY

Coping, resilience & positivity
– lessons from a worldwide pandemic

Indiya Sacha

Indiya Sacha
Life in Lockdown I: The Good, The Bad & The Ugly
Coping, resilience & positivity – lessons from a worldwide pandemic

Cover design: Bas van Tuijl

This book is dedicated to all who struggled their way through lockdown. Mental ill-health is a battle, the anguish and pain of which cannot ever be articulated. It is personal and painful and it kills.

To all of you suffering, I hope that you find the words in these pages comforting and inspiring. You are not alone. There is always light.

Asia, this is for you.

*I heard that we are in the same boat.
But it's not that.
We are in the same storm, but not in the same boat.
Your ship can be shipwrecked and mine might not be.
Or vice versa.
For some, quarantine is optimal: a moment of reflection, or reconnection.
Easy, in flip flops, with a whiskey or tea.
For others, this is a desperate crisis.
For others, it is facing loneliness.
For some, peace, rest time, vacation.
Yet for others, Torture: How am I going to pay my bills?
Some were concerned about a brand of chocolate for Easter (this year there were no rich chocolates).
Others were concerned about the bread for the weekend, or if the noodles would last for a few more days.
Some were in their 'home office'.
Others are looking through trash to survive.
Some want to go back to work because they are running out of money.
Others want to kill those who break the quarantine.
Some need to break the quarantine to stand in line at the banks.
Others to escape.
Others criticise the government for the lines.
Some have experienced the near-death of the virus, some have already lost someone from it, and some believe they are infallible and will be blown away if or when this hits someone they know.
Some have faith in God and expect miracles during 2020. Others say the worse is yet to come. So, friends, we are not in the same boat.
We are going through a time when our perceptions and needs are completely different. And each one will emerge, in his own way, from that storm.
It is very important to see beyond what is seen at first glance. Not just looking, more than looking, seeing.
See beyond the political party, beyond biases, beyond the nose on your face. Do not judge the good life of the other, do not condemn the bad life of the other.
Don't be a judge.
Let us not judge the one who lacks, as well as the one who exceeds him.
We are on different ships looking to survive.
Let everyone navigate their route with respect, empathy and responsibility.*

-Damian Barr, 2020-

CONTENTS

UNPRECEDENTED & UNRELENTING

It's no exaggeration to say that 2020/21 will forever go down as a tumultuous time: the coronavirus/COVID-19 worldwide pandemic; the resultant international lockdown and social distancing; a scary and divisive political era; human rights violations; as well as environmental and accidental catastrophes.

The world has been through the wringer before; World Wars I and II and other pandemics had significant impact on humanity. However, unlike previous pandemics, such as the 1918 Spanish Flu, COVID-19 arrived when international travel was cheap and efficient. We are, quite simply, so used to travelling that we consider it a right, an entitlement. Containing a virus on such an international stage was always going to be nigh on impossible. The world skidded to a halt, our freedoms were curtailed and our lives changed, perhaps irrevocably; only time will tell. Of course, our rights and freedoms have been curtailed before, but usually during times of war. Whilst the horrors of war will always be considered just that, one thing always remained – togetherness. And therein lies the difference with 2020/21; which has been a time of extreme isolation.

THE HIERARCHY OF HUMAN NEED

In times of pain and anguish, of high stress and anxiety, it's a human need to be connected. We're social animals and we thrive off nurture and community. But in 2020 we found ourselves alone and isolated. No visits from friends or family when we were feeling sad or worried; no hugs from those who would normally comfort us. At its worst our loved ones died alone with only a handful of people permitted to attend their funeral. Put simply, 2020 went against every human instinct and the most basic of our human needs.

You may be familiar with Maslow's Hierarchy of Needs – the psychological theory that we have five universal levels of human need? In case you've never heard of it, it goes like this. Maslow believed that there are fundamental needs that must be met in order for us to be fully satisfied and lead a fulfilled life. The more fundamental the need, the lower it is in the hierarchy. It starts with physiological need (for shelter, food, water, sleep, warmth); then safety (personal security, health, employment, property, money); then love and belonging (friendship, family, sense of connection, intimacy); then esteem (self-esteem, respect, recognition, strength, accomplishment, autonomy); and finally, self-actualisation (achieving goals, problem solving, creativity, spirituality, morality, acceptance of fact, spontaneity, lack of prejudice).

Now, the first two levels are the fundamental basic human needs required for survival; if we don't have our physiological needs met we'll die and not having our safety needs met will leave us in a fairly perilous and insecure position. The second two are our psychological needs to feel loved, appreciated and a sense of belonging; if these needs are not met this is where we start to experience poor mental health and well-being, we feel disconnected, lonely, unappreciated, anxious and lacking in control. And finally, our self-actualisation (including transcendency, or spiritual connectedness) needs are where we feel that we've reached our potential, we've achieved what we want to achieve and become all that we want to be.

There's debate around Maslow's theory, but it proves a useful framework for us to better understand the impact of COVID-19 on our individual and collective experiences, because we all have different levels of unmet need, as the (much) shorter poem of Damian Barr aptly concludes:

> *"We are not all in the same boat.*
> *We are all in the same storm.*
> *Some of us are on super-yachts*
> *Some have just the one oar."*

During the pandemic and lockdown, we may have been getting our very bottom layer of physiological needs met but that's pretty much where it ended for some people. These are the people who, in Damian Barr's words, had 'just the one oar'. I realise this sounds a bit morose and possibly even dramatic, but to be frank, it has been for some people. I count myself incredibly lucky to have had my most basic needs met during the pandemic – psychological and safety needs – but others have not been so lucky. Some have lost jobs and struggled financially. Some have had their health seriously compromised, either by COVID-19 or by other ailments that they've either not sought treatment for out of fear or have had treatment and diagnosis delayed due to the overwhelming burden on the health care system. I was fortunate that my basic human needs were met but I struggled thereafter with lack of contact with my loved ones, a lack of connectedness and sense of belonging; I started to feel low, anxious and lonely. And there was absolutely no way in hell that I was going to reach anywhere remotely near self-actualisation since I could rarely motivate myself even to get dressed. I know that I'm not alone in this.

Sure, we were technologically connected every minute of every day but physically and socially we've been completely alone. Whilst we can all lament the pitfalls of social media – and I myself am very aware of the negative impact it can have on mental health, social connections, ability to communicate and so on – but in some ways social media saved us during lockdown. It enabled us to stay connected in the only way we could – virtually. It gave us a sense of solidarity when we couldn't *be* together. But, as time pressed on, the loneliness and disconnect became very real, particularly for people living alone and single parents. So, whilst Maslow's theory has its flaws, it's been a really useful way for me to understand my own experience of lockdown and why it felt the way it did and I began to ponder what others had done to fulfil their needs.

THE POWER OF CONNECTION

The concept of this book came about one day mid-2020 as I was mindlessly scrolling through the social media accounts of friends and family (okay, I'll admit to the odd celebrity too). Regardless of who these people were there was one thing that jumped out at me: some had flourished during lockdown whilst others had languished. I knew this anecdotally from my own personal experience too – I had friends and family who'd absolutely loved lockdown and some who'd really struggled (myself included). What had we all done so differently, I began to wonder?

At the start of the pandemic, I joined a Facebook group called *'View from my Window'* which encouraged members from around the world to share a photo of their view during lockdown. The response was phenomenal and the group grew to over two million members all sharing their views – from beautiful landscapes and seascapes, to gorgeous gardens, to architectural city views and those more 'normal' and less extravagant (a beautiful book – *'View from my Window'* – with just some of these photos and accompanying stories has been published). It truly was magnificent travelling the world and connecting with all these people at a time when the disconnect was so real we couldn't even leave the house. But what really hit me was that people *wanted* to share; they *wanted* to feel part of something bigger as we collectively experienced our enforced social isolation.

A number of different projects have also emerged in the attempt to capture just part of the experience of the worldwide lockdown. Scots author Karen Campbell is working with Dumfries & Galloway based *'Atlas Pandemica'* to capture how the region responded to the pandemic by fictionalising the stories of local authority workers such as teachers and refuse collectors. Perth and Kinross Council have launched the *'Lost/Found'* project to gather the experiences of people across Perthshire on what they had lost and/or found during lockdown. In Crawley, a community project called *'Capturing Lockdown'* has documented in photographs the lives of residents during the pandemic. Tullie House Museum and Art Gallery in Carlisle displayed a similar exhibition of their local area, *'Alone Together: Our community in lockdown 2020'*. Staffordshire Archives and Heritage Service are collecting documents to retell the COVID-19 local story in its project *'Lockdown Memories'*. Hell, even the Duchess of Cambridge is getting in on the action alongside the National Portrait Gallery with a digital exhibition called *'Hold Still'* to illustrate what life was like for people during lockdown.

My local Co-op published a booklet of short statements of how their customers found lockdown. Janey Godley published a summary of her popular very sweary voice-overs of political leaders during the pandemic in *'Frank Get the Door!*

Ma feet are killin me'. There are also a number of books – *'The Lockdown Diary of Tom Cooper'* by Spencer Brown and *'Narratives of the Lockdown'* and *'Narratives from the Lockdown: The Second Wave'* both by G.G. Howells – which attempt to capture the experience of the pandemic and lockdown in fictional tales.

'View from my window' is another example on an international scale; as is the documentary *'Life in Lockdown'* by 16-year-old Octavia Sanger which explores lockdown experiences from a diverse range of people from across the world, available on Amazon Prime. These are just some projects that I've stumbled across; there are no doubt many more throughout the UK and beyond. What all these projects have in common is our human need to connect and share our experiences with one another. These will all be extraordinary reminders of an extraordinary time.

This got me thinking that each of us had our own story to tell about those long months and by telling those stories we might be able to learn from and better understand each other. I'm a writer; I've always found writing about my experience's cathartic and therapeutic (it's a hell of a lot cheaper than therapy too!). And so, I thought, what better way to capture this than to have people write their story; as none of us will have experienced this surreal and traumatic time the same.

At the start of lockdown, I remember telling my kids that this would be a time they'd remember forever – history in the making. Of course, my then eight-year-old boys weren't interested in documenting their time (that would've eaten into their pyjama wearing YouTube or Fortnite marathons after all). I hope that in capturing first-hand lived experiences of this incredibly bizarre time in history, that this book will be something that we can all look back on in years to come. And maybe, just maybe, if such a time comes again, people will understand that they may not be in the same boat but they're not alone, they can get through it and that it's okay to feel however they feel when times are shit and they're doing it tough (I call this the 'shit pit').

I put a call out on social media and invited people to share their experiences for inclusion in this book (okay, I may also have twisted a few arms too). I wanted to show the many human faces of the pandemic – those who're single and those with a partner, those with kids and those without, old and young, employed and unemployed…you get the gist. And so, people wrote their stories and sent them to me, with the agreement I could publish them in 'Life in Lockdown'.

COPING, RESILIENCE & POSITIVITY

In my head this project started out as a book full of experiences with a brief introduction and conclusion but it soon became clear that there was something more within the stories; there were lessons, and lots of them. As the stories came in and I read them – often laughing, crying and nodding simultaneously – it was clear how powerful they were and I decided I'd summarise the messages that were becoming clearer the more I read. There'd be a chapter devoted to individual mental health and well-being and another devoted to addressing some of the collective issues around inequality. More and more stories fell into my inbox and I wrote with gusto. I was excited and passionate that these tales of triumph and heartbreak could help us individually and collectively, even globally. When the manuscript got to 150,000 words and *still* wasn't finished it dawned on me that I either had to restrict what was included (which felt a bit shit as I didn't want to stifle the messages) or I had to think about presenting it differently.

There were clearly two overarching themes: lessons for individual well-being and collective lessons for societal and/or global well-being. This is when the resolution to my *'War & Peace'* problem became obvious – I'd split the book in two: book one would be the individual lessons and book two the collective. And so, the *'Life in Lockdown Duology'* was born. It felt right and fit perfectly with the stories and selecting which stories belonged to which book was easy, it was almost as if they'd been written with two books in mind. This the first in the duology: *'Coping, resilience & positivity'*, and it focuses on individual struggles and the lessons within the pages on how to cope better, build resilience and focus on the positives and the impact on your mental health and well-being.

Writing this book genuinely brought tears to my eyes, it's been an incredibly emotional journey (and naïvely one that I thought would be easy). The stories in these pages are difficult to read. There's happiness, joy, laughter, gratitude and hope. But there's also sorrow, heartbreak, pain, loneliness and the omnipresent limbo that's been 2020/21. None are completely negative, just as none are all sunshine and roses. They are raw and honest and true. They are the good times and the bad times, warts and all.

The most powerful thing about these stories is the knowledge that these are *real* people's experiences; they've been written by *real* people. They are not made up, they are not fictionalised, they are their real lives and they are in their own words. What they show is that we are never alone in life's difficulties. It doesn't help your difficulties any, I know, but when I was in the shit pit I took a lot of comfort in reading these stories and recognising the strength and resilience of these amazing people, even if, at the time, they didn't see it themselves.

As I received the stories one by one, each person thanked me. Not for putting their story in this book, but because of what the process of writing their story involved. Some had found it therapeutic, some said it had given them a sense of perspective, some said it made them realise the past year hadn't been as bad as they thought it had and others said it made them realise their emotional strength. Their stories gave me perspective, strength and optimism that I, too, could come out of the darkness into the light.

The stories in the pages of this book come from a range of different perspectives. Some people loved their experience of lockdown, some hated it and suffered significantly. There are stories from people living alone, people who live with their partners and those living with family. There are stories from young people, older people, healthy people and those who had to shield. There are stories from those who went through relationship breakdowns, those who were bereaved and those who got engaged and had babies. There are stories from those who were employed, unemployed, retired, students and self-employed, those working from home and those who were furloughed. I am forever grateful to all these people for sharing their experiences – good and bad – with such candour. They are stories of coping, resilience and positivity. But most of all, they are stories of strength. They are stories of hope.

PART 1

LIFE IN LOCKDOWN:
THE GOOD, THE BAD & THE UGLY

ADULTHOOD ON HOLD

You could say we saw it coming. As soon as Ireland announced they were closing schools, the sixth-year social area felt a bit more special, looked a bit more nostalgic – even classes seemed a bit more interesting. As if our head teacher's wishes had come true, sixth year attendance reached an all-time high, fewer McDonald's trips in free periods and more social area chit chat, everyone sitting tight for the lurking announcement. A few weeks previous the thought of schools closing seemed nothing but whimsical and barbaric. I remember my biology teacher prepping us 'just in case' we had to resort to online learning. Now, teachers were beginning to frantically gather evidence, squeezing every timed essay out of us before it was too late. Sure enough, Wednesday came. Everyone gathered round a phone screen in the social area whilst Mr Swinney pronounced: schools are closing.

As if by instinct there has always been a glimmer of glee and giddiness when schools close, like snow days or polling days – it felt good. Yet, this time the bubbles in our tummies fizzed into tears running down our eyes. And so began the hugs from people you thought would never make amends and the paparazzi of each other's faces, knowing the timeless importance of each snap. The excitement of the infamous last day we were promised for the last thirteen years vanishing; no yearbooks, karaoke machine or photo booth. The day, slipping out of our close grasp.

Schools closing was one thing, but the announcement of the SQA exams being cancelled was a whole new level of emotion for teachers and pupils alike. I've never seen a corridor like the one I saw ten minutes after the announcement. The *'ugh they're only prelims'* mantra became suddenly twisted, the painstaking hours spent re-writing notes or completing hundreds of past paper questions became quickly meaningless, conditional university offers or meeting entry requirements instantaneously jeopardised. To put it frankly, it was devastating, despite the deceiving 'no exams!'

Yet quickly everyone's devastation was shoved to one side and what was meant to be a bog-standard Friday, became a mish-mash of makeshift pranks, shirt signing and goodbyes. It was not what we wanted, but it was something. Of course, all decisions were correct, and everyone understood our sadness was trivial in the grand scheme of things.

School became distant, yet it still seemed very much relevant. Prom was still in question, our £400 prom dresses clung to the hope that they could fulfil their destiny. Regular zoom quizzes and parties attempted to impersonate the rite of passage that is an eighteenth birthday and experiencing the world of nightlife for the first time. Again, it was not what we wanted, but it was something. As for sixth year holidays however, not even zoom could mimic them...and so, began the tensions and tireless time spent on refunds and packing away our bikinis. That being said, most importantly everybody was still together, every school clique and friendship was still there, 'being in it together' was a comfort blanket to hide from the realities of the pandemic and those waiting for us outside of our adolescence. Nobody was clubbing, partying or ordering drinks, we were all going through it together.

But then, university came. I decided to take a gap year from my studies; due to going to university in America, it seemed sensible, yet, none of my friends made the same decision. The comfort blanket in the world of uncertainty was quickly ripped away. I can only describe it as being ships in a harbour, with little people screaming and smiling sail away, but mine doesn't start. The concept of COVID restrictions for them, quickly became something they left at port. Hall parties, nights out in the city, new friends, life experience and independence. Of course, for them I was happy, but I couldn't help my feeling of sadness that my life was on hold, whilst theirs was just getting started. I still lived with my parents, followed the rules and so the loneliness a lockdown brings started to encapsulate me. Even so, I felt for my friends giving up their 'freshers' week, in person lectures and a proper opportunity to explore their new cities. It was not what they had dreamed university to be.

For me, my home-town upbringing and school era has not yet been closed. It never received closure, or a proper send off and now everyone else has seemingly moved on, I don't think it ever will. So, I suppose I will always feel a little youthful, my teenage years didn't get to live like they should have. Whether this spurs me to go clubbing when I'm 80 or leads me down a path of teetotal-ness and early nights, it will always be an unclosed era of my life.

I was lucky to find a job and since I have worked throughout the zig zag of restrictions. It's not the best, putting parcels on a shelf all night, but it keeps me busy and occupied. Even seeing people in the flesh has been a luxury. If not working you will find me, like the others, going on daily walks, cleaning my room, zooming some friends. A year which could not be more different to the one which was meant to be, and the one I had worked so hard for: Boston, new friends, parties, university. Yet I have adapted to this life, it was not what I wanted, but it was something.

With hopes of summer 2021 returning to the 'old normal', things are looking up. I cannot wait to experience, what some might regard as the upside of adulthood: ordering drinks for the first time, clubbing, going away with friends. Despite this, I am nervous to have yet another dramatic change to the 'new normal' living. Yes, the year(s) of lockdown has not been great, but I've created my own new normal, wrapped myself in a new comfort blanket, which is about to be ripped away again.

Generally, I've felt okay over the lockdown as I have a very supportive family and have kept myself from spiralling by working. I've met people at work who have made life seem a bit more normal. If I've learnt anything it's definitely not to take things for granted, and how it's important to take time for yourself and not get swept away by the business of life.

LOCKDOWN LONELINESS

Lockdown was pretty tough for me. I am a single mum of three. Being stuck in the house with the children trying to home school, keep them amused and prevent them from killing each other felt, most of the time, impossible. It left little time for me to focus on keeping myself sane and upbeat. Naturally something had to give and it always seemed to be me and my needs to stay well.

I have no family close by and many days I did not see another adult at all. I did not see my family at all in 2020 and I guess it will be a while yet before I see them again. I have a lot of friends in the local area (and beyond) and usually am quite sociable – meeting up for coffee, popping into their houses for a catch up or having a boozy night at one of their houses or in the pub. A group of us normally go away abroad on a long weekend once a year too. The inability to see friends in person, talk to them when I needed to and cry with them when I needed to was awful.

I have a boyfriend who lives an hour away from me in a different local authority area of Scotland, so we were not able see each other for three months because of the social distancing and travel restrictions in place. That was very tough, probably the part I found the hardest. I missed seeing him very much – but I also missed his family, who had become part of my life. Things are still not the same because, at the time I write this, we are still under restrictions – we do not see each other nearly as much as we used to and this is a continual struggle.

It makes me sad to say that the highlight of my week became the weekly shop, as there I at least got to speak to another adult. I also found that going outside for my one permissible walk or run became very valuable as it was often the only time I would get peace away from the children. With the exception of a few days here and there, I did not get any real or lasting respite from the kids and my usual support network wasn't there anymore. Like everyone else, I phoned people, I Zoomed and Skyped and House Partied and the like, but it isn't the same. When you're feeling lonely and stressed with the kids and needing a break – a video call or 'party' doesn't really make a difference, beyond a few hours of offloading verbally and laughing. It's not the same as physically getting to see a friend or getting out of the house or getting a hug. I was stressed doing it all alone with the kids. I missed my boyfriend terribly. I lost – at least physically – my support network. Like everyone, in particular single parents, I was completely isolated yet with additional pressures I wasn't prepared for.

My mental health has really suffered because of lockdown and continues to do so. I think it will take a long time for me to recover from this. I felt very isolated and alone most of the time. Even now, almost a year after the first national lockdown, I am still feeling the effects and do not feel like I am back to my pre-lockdown self. When restrictions started to be lifted after the initial lockdown and we were able to travel a bit more I found that, despite my loneliness and previous desperation to get out of the house, I really didn't want to. The first time I went into the town where, before lockdown, I would go once a week for a coffee and a nose around the shops I found that I hated it – I managed only two sips of my coffee before I left the coffee shop, I hardly went into any shops – I couldn't wait to go home again. The more I've done this – and I had to force myself to – it is getting easier. It saddens me that what was once an enjoyable escape is now really hard, almost a chore, and I head home as soon as I can.

I definitely have anxiety now which I never really had before, my sleep is completely messed up and I am still trying to get myself back to who I was before this all happened. I have found the constant changing of rules, regulations and restrictions has been tough, and when a new announcement is due to come out, my anxiety rockets and I spend much of my days crying and over thinking about potential new restrictions and possible consequences of those.

So many things that I was looking forward to have been cancelled and those that are still going ahead are not the same and actually more stressful than enjoyable. In the latter half of 2020 I should have been away to the Dominican Republic for a 10 night 5* all-inclusive holiday with my boyfriend for a family wedding but it was cancelled. I had so been looking forward to it as a real break away from life and a chance for my boyfriend and I to really spend some quality time together. But that didn't happen and it really knocked me sideways for a while. I understood why it had to be this way, but it didn't make the disappointment any easier. When you look forward to something as much as that, something you've never had the chance to do before, it crushes you. I had already lost so much due to lockdown; it was almost like this was the last straw for a while.

The only good thing to come out of lockdown is that I think my boyfriend and I are closer now – it has made us realise how much we mean to each other and how important we are in each other's lives. Also, before all of this I really hadn't realised how much a part of my life his family had become and how much I love spending time with them.

All this has made me realise how much I like routine, how much I like certain aspects of my life to be predictable and safe. But also, how much I need those treats and the time away from my children, time with other adults, time to be me rather than just being 'mum'.

Self-care wasn't really something I did a lot of in the first lockdown, mainly due to not getting much time to myself. One thing I did start doing regularly was taking a bath which gave me 30 minutes to an hour locked away on my own (although that didn't stop my children from knocking on the door or arguing). Getting out to walk my dog or go for a run helped but ultimately, I knew that I needed help from my doctor and so after a discussion I was advised to go on anti-depressants. I also used the listening service at my GP surgery which helped as it let me 'offload' in confidence. When I did have childfree time, I was either spending it at my partner's house (when allowed) or, when we were still under strict restrictions, keeping myself busy doing jobs around the house.

I lost my inclination to do any crafts or reading during lockdown. Normally crafting or reading is something I do regularly, but I just didn't have the headspace or concentration to do any. I also found myself eating a lot more than I normally would, mainly because of emotional eating and boredom.

The second time round in lockdown I'm trying to keep some sort of routine and trying to find time to myself – even if it is only ten minutes to shut my bedroom door and taking time to just relax and breathe. I make a point of talking to friends and family, I'm sharing how I'm feeling – the highs *and* the lows – because even a virtual catch up is still a catch up. I think the most important thing during lockdown, or isolation, is to look after yourself – after all, as one of my favourite sayings goes: 'you can't pour from an empty cup'.

BLURRED LINES & HEALTH ANXIETY: WHEN CAN WE LIVE THE WAY WE WANT TO LIVE?

To be honest when I first heard the news of coronavirus heading our way I didn't give it a massive amount of thought, imagined it would blow over quickly. How I was so wrong! When it was announced we were going into lock down in March 2020 for three weeks I instantly thought *'ok, that's not too long and it will actually be quite nice for us to spend time as a family at home together'*; something we don't do as my husband has his own business and never takes quality time off just to spend it at home. *'Yippee,'* I thought, *'I will get things done around the house!'*

Early on we started to hear of folk running to the shops buying up everything and the shelves left bare. I was thinking to myself *'seriously people, just take what you need'* and couldn't believe it when I went to the local shop and it was sparse, although I did find myself – like everyone else – picking up long life milk and bread mix (still in my cupboard to the present day). Peer pressure kicked in!

I continued to work my usual shifts as a midwife and going to work made things feel more normal in a way, despite the use of PPE and continuous hand washing and hand gel use. However, I did initially have huge anxiety about catching

COVID-19 and giving it to my family or that I would be one of the random cases of a healthy woman dying of the virus. I do suffer from health-related anxiety and the pandemic reignited it so I had to try and self-manage my anxiety which I managed, although I think a lot of this was natural due to the passing of time.

At work, I could initially feel a huge amount of anxiety and fear among the women as we couldn't give them any answers really to what they really wanted to know; that if they were to catch COVID-19 that themselves and their baby would be okay. It was all very unknown and there were very few reported infections in pregnant woman around the world at that time so it was a complete unknown. One of my ladies chose not to continue with her pregnancy as she just felt overwhelmed with the thought of lockdown and the potential implications of COVID-19 – health wise, on the antenatal care and on delivery – and honestly felt it was the only option for her at that time. It wasn't an easy decision for her but suffering from health anxiety as I do I completely understood her concern.

Women's partners are not allowed to attend antenatal appointments and this is very difficult for some women who feel almost as if this journey is one they are on alone. This was particularly the case during the period that partners were not allowed in for ultrasound appointments, were only allowed to be at the birth during active labour and were only allowed to stay for limited time after the birth. This was hard to watch as many women needed their partners' support and we found that the women were needing to talk to us for longer as often we were the only other person – besides their partner – that they were seeing from week to week.

During the first lockdown we had no cases of COVID-19 in pregnant women but this has changed during the second peak and more women have become infected with the virus which has heightened the impact of it on the services we're able to provide. We have scaled back face-to-face contact appointments and visits at home unless absolutely necessary but we are always there for support on the phone. I do feel very lucky to be able to continue going to my work and being able to support women during this challenging time – a time that shouldn't be full of worry or health-related anxiety.

After the baby is born and we are doing home visits it feels very different than it did pre-COVID. Under normal circumstances extended family are there and women talk of family and friends visiting. But that's all had to stop and that can feel lonely for some. On the other hand, for a lot of women I think the pressure of having no one else in the house and just themselves, their partner and other children, allows them to relax and have time to bond as a close family unit. They don't have the worry of keeping the house clean, having nice biscuits in for a cup of tea for visitors or actually being up and dressed. Many of the women with older children have actually told me that it feels so much better this time round, so I think that many new mums do feel a sense of pressure to welcome family and friends into their home in the very early days. COVID-19 and the lockdown has relieved this pressure. It's not ideal for everyone, but I think most new mums have welcomed the time to relax into having a new baby at home. That is quite nice to see as a midwife and might go some way to kind of balance out the negative impacts of the restrictions antenatally and during the birth.

Having my children at home and having quality time as a family on the days when I was at work seemed great, but I remember the feeling when I was at work and a friend texted me to say she had just heard that the schools would be closed until August. I instantly felt a sense of doom! Having a six and nine-year-old at home 24/7 I knew was going to be a challenge!

Nearly a year into it and we have had good days and bad days. There are days where we don't really want to get out of bed but, as time has gone on, we are just learning to roll with them.

The weather in summer 2020 made a huge difference during the first lockdown as we spent a massive amount of time outside in the garden, having BBQ's and going on walks and cycles – something we made sure to do every day and this was a real positive that came from lockdown. Initially my husband and I treated it like it was a bit of a holiday – we drank more and ate more – but as the realisation of an extended lock down hit us we decided that we needed to exercise more. We both took up running again and for me it was an escape from the house. Now, on the odd day when my husband is now able to work again, he comes home to find me standing with all my running gear on ready to escape as soon as he walks in the door.

I am definitely not a natural teacher when it comes to the children's learning and some days I just have to walk away and give myself a breather and a lot of counting back from 10 has been required on occasion! I admit to finding it difficult to control the usage of technology for my children. Because of home schooling we have had to introduce it into our lives far more than we ever used it before which I have found challenging. As it is the way the school is communicating with us and the children it's impossible to avoid – as much as I try to print work off its just impossible to avoid it and we do need to access it every day. I think this has blurred the lines a bit too much between home and school which will require a lot of scaling back as we get back to a more normal life!

The children are really missing their friends and school routines and especially their sports clubs, particularly my son who plays football. This is vital for his health and wellbeing and I've really noticed how much he's missing it. Grandparents are such a huge part of my children's lives and not being able to see them properly for nearly a year has been so hard on everyone. They both get so much from spending quality time with them and out of everything I think this is what we have missed the most – a hug is so important and something we definitely took for granted before which is something I'll never do again!

Lockdown has made me realise how much I enjoy time away from my normal routine. I have really missed our holidays as a family, either abroad or to our cottage in Ireland. I have also really missed seeing friends and, as time goes on, this is getting harder and harder – we are sociable beings and this is not a way to live. I really am longing for things to get better so we can reintroduce social gatherings.

As a midwife I was a priority for getting the vaccine and, at the time I write this, I have had my first COVID-19 vaccine and am waiting to get my second dose. I pray that these vaccines and the vaccination programme works so that we can get back to some form of normality as we go through 2021. Another year of lockdown doesn't bear thinking about.

Looking ahead there are so many things we took for granted: seeing family; hugs; taking time to see friends; watching the children do their sports; meeting for a coffee; going to the non-essential shop; soft play; and holidays. That said, I know how lucky I am to have a secure job as so many people do not have that security – or have lost it due to lockdown – and the impact of this will only become more noticeable as normal life begins to resume again.

COVID-19 without doubt, like everyone else, impacted significantly on my family and how we live our life. We have enjoyed aspects of it and definitely become healthier and become a closer family unit. But we are missing family and friends so much and it's becoming increasingly difficult to stay away from them. Our children need school and their clubs and activities – I am not designed to be a home school teacher! We enjoy each other's company as a family of four but are eagerly awaiting the restrictions to be lifted and a more normal life.

Being a midwife during the pandemic has definitely increased my anxiety but I have learnt to deal with it better and I consider myself lucky to be able to talk to and support women during this strange time. Really, I have learnt never to take normal things for granted. I just pray, now, that the roll out of the vaccines is enough to allow us to live the way we want to live.

GREAT INTENTIONS, NETFLIX & WINE

Lockdown happened at a really tough time for me. In the latter half of 2019 I had a bit of an emotional breakdown. I had to deal with the issues that I'd been burying, I had to learn to ask for help, I had to rely on others and I had to learn what it was like to be alone. I had struggled with adjusting to being a single parent and the absence of my children when they were with their dad. The silence was thundering; the emptiness all-encompassing. By the end of 2019 I was finally in a place of…not contentment, but acceptance. I was getting used to being on my own and my new life. I figured that taking anti-anxiety and antidepressant medication alone wasn't going to help me and that I needed to make some lifestyle changes so, at the start of 2020, I gave up alcohol. Now this was no easy feat – I've drank since I was in my late (okay mid) teens and tend to rely on alcohol when I'm stressed. My friends and I like nothing more than a catch up with copious amounts of Prosecco, wine and gin. So, yeah, giving up was tough. But boy did I feel better for it. My head was no longer in a fog, I was productive, I was motivated, I was happy. I was hopeful for a happy future. Finally! I'd waited so long to feel like this and, after a few years of bleak despair, I was relieved.

I was three months with no alcohol when it was announced that the UK would go into a national lockdown on 23rd March 2020. I knew it was coming, we'd seen China, Italy, France and Spain go through the same thing in the weeks before. I have to admit that at the start it was exciting. Here we were, in the middle of a pandemic, and we didn't have to go in to work and the kids didn't have to go to school. It seemed, in my naivety, that we were getting one long holiday. Some much needed downtime. No more rushing around, stressing about getting to work or getting the kids up for school. Who wouldn't want that?

I had such wonderful plans at the start of lockdown. I was going to decorate my bedroom. I was going to paint the living room. I was going to cook lovely meals. I was going to get fit and healthy. I was going to stick to the home-schooling. I was going to go for a daily walk. I was going to read lots of books. I was going to do lots of things. What did I do? Very little. Although I did make a huge dent in my Netflix and Amazon Prime viewing list.

Fast-forward and that extended holiday had turned into something mentally destructive. I gave up on my sober life because, well, why not? I didn't have to go anywhere. I didn't have to drive anywhere. I didn't have to put a 'face' on for anyone else. I didn't have any appointments to attend. Hell, I didn't even have to get dressed. I was lost. Flailing in one everlasting dreaded Sunday. I'd call it Groundhog Day but actually it was worse – Groundhog Day in the same four walls with no other human contact bar my kids (if the screenwriters had foretold this back in 1993, Bill Murray would've had a much worse time of it!). So, I fell back into old habits and got tucked into the good old emotional suppressor – wine! It's not like I was drinking all the time or in the morning or anything, but I was drinking more than was healthy – disconnection and boredom are not a good combination. I'm not exaggerating when I say it was hell. I fell back into the state of anxiety and depression I'd fought so hard to get out of. And I know I'm not the only one who went down this road.

My kids' dad still had to go out to work whilst I was able to work from home. Being a civil servant was a godsend really as my employer was very understanding, my boss even more so and I didn't experience any reduction in income. But, because my boys' dad was away working they stayed with me Monday through Friday and then stayed with him every weekend. This meant I had to work whilst home schooling loud and energetic twin boys. My work required a fair amount of concentration and the information is incredibly sensitive, traumatic and highly confidential. Add in the obligatory video meetings and phone calls and it was impossible to get anywhere very fast with work. I said as much to my boss one day a few weeks in, telling her – rather optimistically in hindsight – that I'd work at weekends when the boys were at their dad's. Eh? *'Nope',* my brain and body said come Friday, *'I don't think so!'* By the time they were collected on Friday evening I was utterly exhausted. I couldn't even watch anything more than rubbish TV and certainly nothing that required even a modicum of brain power. I basically slept, ate, and stared at the TV all weekend, every weekend (oh, and drank wine…lots of wine).

Given I wasn't going anywhere, doing anything or socialising, I envisaged I'd save myself a pile of money. How wrong could I be? Having my boys at home all day cost me an arm and a leg. Seriously, I'm surprised I'm not bankrupt. These kids ate every hour of every day, with snacks in between. I could hardly keep them fed. Alongside trying to do some form of educational activities, keeping them from killing each other, keeping them fed and watered was a full-time job in itself. All whilst cooped up in a small two-bedroom flat (which needs a lot of DIY and renovation), 'working' and trying to keep my own spirits up. Talk about a recipe for mental health disaster!

The worst thing though was being so completely alone. Being a single parent is hard but being a single parent alone during lockdown was horrendous – I don't think I can articulate just how hard it was. At a time when I yearned for human connection, being completely isolated was incredibly depressing. I'm not the only one. The amount of posts on social media from folk I knew and folk I didn't just highlighted how lonely single people felt. The only human contact I had – besides my children – was with my ex. Thankfully we are great friends and he did have to give me a hug or two when I was really down (I may have cried on his knee once or twice), but that isn't the same as getting a hug from a close confidante, family member, friend or partner. Video calls didn't even come close to buoying my spirits or making me feel connected to the people I cared about the most.

Early(ish) in lockdown a friendship with an old school friend came to an end too. It had been coming for a while but lockdown and the pandemic brought to the fore our moral differences and it became pretty clear we were no longer good for each other. It was hard and quite sad as this was someone who'd been part of my life and a very close friend since school. I think this would've happened anyway and, to be honest, was probably overdue, but the emotional circumstances of 2020 definitely sped the end of our friendship and 2020 was hard enough as it was without added heartache.

During lockdown, my dad became homeless due to a relationship breakdown. His homelessness, his physical health (which required him to shield during lockdown) and his deteriorating mental health and not looking after himself resulted in him being hospitalised numerous times – during a time we were unable to travel, unable to visit and unable to speak face-to-face with the many hospitals, social workers, homeless officers and so on. Try sorting all of that out over the phone. It was hellish. Stressful. Anxiety invoking. All whilst working, looking after the kids (home school went out the window!) and the pressures of daily life. Then my 89-year-old gran became very unwell just before Christmas and my mum was very worried about her. It's hard not to be able to give someone a hug when you're under such emotional pressure, particularly those who're doing it tough.

So, the cycle of being alone, being stressed, being depressed, eating rubbish, drinking wine, not stimulating my brain and not exercising took its toll – I put on weight, I was continually exhausted and I was utterly depressed. Try as I might I just couldn't get out of that revolving door of misery. Anyone who's struggled with their mental health will understand what I mean.

The start of 2021 brought another lockdown. I made a very conscious decision not to fall back into the habits of 2020 – I couldn't. I genuinely didn't think I'd cope if I lived this lockdown the same as the last. I've given up alcohol again and my mood lifted within days. I go out for walks. I'm cooking again and my boys and I eat meals together at the table. I keep on top of the housework. I de-cluttered. I put away technology and have picked up the huge pile of books beside my bed (I even try not to video call, unless it's for work). I focus on my boys. I focus on my work. I've re-committed to projects I'd neglected in 2020. I've started again with the DIY. The TV isn't always on. I've got to grips with my finances (even though it's not so nice seeing it in black and white – am I the only one who spent a fortune online shopping out of boredom?). I'm focusing on my well-being. The choice I've made to change my behaviour means 2021 feels positive, hopeful and I feel content and, dare I say it, optimistic. Yes, the situation hasn't really changed since 2020, but there are vaccines and there's an end in sight (although who knows when). The biggest change though has been my mindset.

What I have found difficult this time round is working and home schooling. In the latter half of 2020 I got a promotion.

This was a job I really wanted, am very enthusiastic about and fits with my long-term goals. My weekly hours increased, as have my responsibilities. But I love it. I'm busy and motivated and thoroughly believe in and am passionate about what I'm doing. This means; however, I have less time to devote to home schooling. As my children are fairly young I've made a conscious decision that we will not necessarily follow the work set by their teacher. Instead we follow our own path – we do educational tasks but we also focus on looking after ourselves and they help me to cook, clean and tidy (life skills are important too!). This works for us, but I do feel guilty at not sticking to the prescribed tasks even though I know it isn't worth grinding myself into the ground with stress. Instead I'm teaching them life skills, resilience and how to look after themselves which, given the situation we've found ourselves in with COVID, is no bad thing to impart. I do, however, make them attend live class Teams meetings with the teacher twice a week. These are not for learning, but keeping in contact with their teacher and peers which I think is very important. But my goodness, if you think a work Teams meeting is awkward and chaotic you should just listen to a bunch of nine-year-old's…I'm often crying with laughter. Just today they were all discussing their pets with the teacher (who is new and only started teaching their class today) and one of the wee lads says clear as day: *'d'you want to see my cat? He looks like he's on drugs'.* I couldn't hold in the laughter – even my boys were in stitches – and my phone went crazy as all the parents messaged each other as we all guffawed from our own homes. I dread to think what the teacher thought and the deputy head who was also on the call! Still, it gave the parents a laugh – it's the little things!!

Both myself and my boys' dad are category two key workers (and both single parents) so we're entitled to places in the local school 'hub' for our boys. However, we haven't been able to get them a place as the 'hub' admission is very strict, despite government guidance to the contrary. I've heard of many secondary school teachers who need to teach live online and even a vaccine scientist working on the COVID-19 vaccine who aren't able to get her child into a 'hub'! I don't know how they manage as, like many parents, I've lost count of the amount of times I've had to leave a meeting because the kids are demanding food, juice, are fighting or just jumping around in the background loving the interaction with the outside world. I thank my lucky stars that my employer has been understanding but I know many people whose employers haven't and who expected them to perform the same as they would pre-pandemic. I can only imagine the pressure.

In mid-January 2021, my dad passed away after his difficult few months health-wise and after a few months in a homeless hostel. My sister (who was amazing at helping dad during this time as I couldn't because of my kids who'd been at school and mixing with friends and potentially exposed to the virus) eventually settled him into supported accommodation with a care package to meet his needs. Unfortunately, he was only there for five days before he died. I hadn't seen him for four months because I didn't want to risk passing the virus to him due to his heart and chronic lung conditions. The Wednesday before my dad died my sister phoned after being with my dad and said that she didn't think he had long left as he was increasingly struggling with his breathing. I was worried about passing him the virus and she told me that she really didn't think it mattered anymore. We arranged to go out together on Friday afternoon. I was just about to leave the house on Friday when she phoned me to tell me he'd been found dead by the carers that morning. I'm beyond grateful to my sister who'd put up pictures of us and his grandchildren; at least I know he had warm and loving faces whilst he struggled alone completely devoid of all physical contact. But, my dad died alone on his sofa in a flat he'd only just moved into after months of homelessness.

My poor sister, who struggles with her own mental health and alcohol dependency, had only just moved him in – arranging for all the furniture and so on – had seven days to clear the flat. Seven fucking days. She'd only moved him in five days earlier, after spending a good month trying to get a social worker and social care package in place. She'd done all of this, stayed with him until two days before he died to settle him in, then lost her dad and had to clear it and return the keys within seven days or face financial penalty. All iterated to her in standard letters. There was no consideration of the extenuating circumstances and the impact that would have. Standard fucking letters! I'm sorry, but that's fucked up, even without the added stress and complication of a pandemic it's a disgrace and inhumane. Housing and adult social care really need to buck up their ideas and start to think about their corporate social responsibility and how they communicate with the bereaved.

The last time I properly saw my dad was in February 2020 when me and my boys went to stay to celebrate a late Christmas. Although I know that my reasons for not seeing him in the year before he died were rational and I was adhering to the restrictions, I don't know if I'll ever be content that I didn't see him or wasn't there for him in his last few months and I'll always think back to the last time I saw him on his birthday in September and how neither my boys or I gave him a hug (in fact, I'm crying just writing this). In normal circumstances, bereavement comes with comfort from friends and family, but in the midst of a pandemic and a strict lockdown, when dad died my sister and I were alone. I told my oldest and bestest friends – who all knew my dad – that he was gone on the phone and wasn't able to go see them for a much-needed shoulder to cry on. Then came the funeral arrangements, awful at the best of times, but even more painful during COVID because of the incredibly difficult decisions to be made. Having watched a funeral via live link, I was acutely aware how distressing funerals were with the restrictions. After a lot of heartache, tears, terse and emotive discussions and internal deliberating (and a few shouty arguments and hung up phone calls) we organised a direct cremation for dad. We'll hold a gathering when the pandemic is over to celebrate his life and scatter his ashes in a place he loved. I've really struggled with this decision, and at times I've felt heartless and an awful daughter (I suspect this is something I will now have to live with for the rest of my life). But I know that a half-arsed funeral where everyone has masks on and has to sit apart is the shittiest way you could ever say goodbye. But it really hurt not being able to give my dad a goodbye at the time, like there's no closure and we didn't care.

One day he's there, the next he's not. He was never a big conversationalist so phone calls were brief and few and far between. Because of COVID, we hadn't seen him in such a long time and had no plans to see him in the near future. So, my dad is gone but my life doesn't feel any different, except every time I open my wardrobe I see the box containing his ashes which we can't scatter because of the restrictions. We weren't able to say goodbye two months ago and we likely won't be able to scatter his ashes together for another year. It'll be over a year before we can say our goodbyes. I honestly don't think I can grieve properly because he's not actually gone from my life at the moment as we've lived in isolation for a year and will continue to live in isolation until this is over. My dad's gone but there's no hole. I can't tell you how wrong it feels and I don't think I'll ever really grieve properly for him because of the virus. The restrictions on saying goodbyes and funerals is one of the cruellest aspects of lockdown and I didn't realise it until I was the one figuring out how to say goodbye.

As hard as it's been, lockdown did bring some benefits. Having my boys with me so much whilst trying to work from home has made me appreciate the times they're with their dad. I've come to love my peaceful empty days with nobody else to worry about besides myself. I now love being home alone. My own company is actually, I've discovered, pretty good. Perhaps the downside might actually be that I like my own company too much now. I've always been a sociable extrovert and have a number of very close friends and a wider group of friends who I can rely on. I've missed them all terribly during lockdown and I do actually worry that, when the world returns to 'normal', that I will struggle to become sociable again, so set in my isolated ways I've become.

For my birthday in December 2020, my mum took me to a hotel for the night, just us. We stayed in the hotel, had a lovely meal, two wonderful swims (I hadn't realised how much I missed swimming!) and a night away from the four walls we'd been stuck in for months. It was glorious, even if it was just three miles away from her home. The following week we went back into a strict lockdown following a significant increase in infection rate due to a new, more virulent strain, of COVID-19. Then, the week before Christmas, my boys were two of 122 children in their school who had to isolate over Christmas due to being close contacts of five positive cases. Thankfully, that night away with mum gave me the respite I needed to recharge my batteries to cope with two hyper children unable to leave the confines of our tiny wee two-bedroom flat. No material gift would've provided that. So, yeah, all that 'stuff' that was important before has become irrelevant in the grand scheme of things. Christmas 2020 was a different affair; stuck home due to the kids' isolation I spent it with my ex and our kids. It was relaxed, there was no traipsing from one house to another, there were few gifts, no pressure, none of the family politics and no stress. It's a lesson I've learnt for the future – that Christmas needn't be a big fancy convoluted affair with heaps of meaningless gifts and hours spent slaving away in the kitchen.

2021 started positively and losing dad hasn't derailed me. If anything, it's motivated me not to fall back into old habits. My dad was a recovering alcoholic, had two terminal health conditions and was only in his early sixties when he died. If he'd passed away in 2020 I'd have gone straight to the shop for a couple of bottles of wine and drank them alone, crying and feeling like shit the next day, physically and emotionally. But I didn't. I want my life to improve and I know that it starts with better choices. I've found myself committing to getting healthier and to achieving my career and creative goals. Dad dying has reinforced that I need to maintain the positive changes I've made and I now possess reinforced enthusiasm.

There are many things in my life that I'm grateful for but I often forget them in the day to day grind. Despite the difficulty, lockdown has made me realise how important the simple things are. What I'm grateful for isn't the fanciest clothes, or the biggest house or the expensive car. What lockdown has done is reinforce my belief that those things mean nothing. It's the small things, things you can't touch, that I'm truly grateful for. When the first lockdown was eased slightly I can't tell you how amazing it was to go into a friend's house for a coffee, or stay at my mums for the night, or go wild camping locally with friends (even though it rained, the midges were horrendous and we got told off by the Countryside Ranger!). Those things are worth more than any material goods.

I'm grateful the rest of my family are healthy and my friends are well. I'm grateful for my friends and family, who know as soon as I say 'hi' whether I'm needing a friendly ear. I'm grateful to my ex for supporting me and giving me a hug during lockdown when I couldn't get one from anyone else. I'm grateful that I have an understanding employer and have been able to work from home and not suffer financially. I'm grateful for my incredibly supportive colleagues. I'm grateful that my boys experienced a 'great' and 'awesome' lockdown (particularly Christmas apparently, which was their 'best ever'!). I'm grateful that I live in a beautiful rural area where I can get out and enjoy nature. I'm grateful for the most amazing view I have from my flat that I marvel at every day. I'm grateful for the sunshine that floods in the windows and makes me feel optimistic. I'm grateful for the rain and snow that makes me feel còsagach (the Scots version of hygge) indoors. I'm grateful for social media and technology that's kept me connected. I'm grateful for my cats who've cuddled and entertained me in equal measure. I'm grateful for the wealth of entertainment at my fingertips.

I could go on, but you get the picture. What I'm grateful for can't be bought (well, some of it can, but they're pretty small) and human connection is our most important need – that is my most significant takeaway from lockdown that I will carry for the rest of my life. The rest of the shit? Well, that really doesn't matter much at all.

LOST IN LOCKDOWN:
I DIDN'T WANT TO BE HERE

I can remember the day we went into our first lockdown well – the day we were sent home from work when it was declared. I remember the panic I felt when I went to the supermarket to get some food but there was nothing left on the shelves! I really was worried and panicking that we'd run out of food! There had been talk of the lockdown happening before so everyone picked up their stock of food and I'd left it too late. I don't think I'd thought it was that big a deal until then.

Before lockdown my life was already in turmoil as three months before my 16-year-old son told me he was moving out and in with his gran and grandad! And he wasn't asking; he was telling me and his bags were already packed! I was absolutely heartbroken; he's my only child and it had always just been him and I and we were really close what with it just having been the two of us. I didn't see it coming at all. It was completely out of nowhere. After that I fell into a really deep and dark depression.

When the first lockdown came I was already low so I was completely lost. Before lockdown my son wasn't around and I was alone in the house but at least I could see him. So, lockdown made that worse cause I wasn't even able to have him round or go visit. I was worried sick too as he has asthma, and because he wasn't with me I didn't know if he was okay or how safe he was. I knew that if he did get coronavirus then he would be really ill and I couldn't stand the thought of not being there if that happened. It was really, really hard because I wasn't able to keep an eye on him or look after him.

When lockdown first happened and we were all given laptops to work from home, I thought that it would be great working from home. It didn't take long for me to figure out it wasn't good for me, and I didn't enjoy it at all. I am a very chatty and sociable person and get on really well with everyone and I found that I really missed my colleagues, friends and the social side of going to work every day. I hadn't realised how much actually going to work was to me.

Work-wise things were really hard during lockdown and I was inundated with emails every day and I was hit with lists and lists of things to do. When lockdown happened I was still pretty new to the job and I sometimes felt like I couldn't ask if I was stuck with something as we only ever got in touch with each other by email. This went on for a good few months and I felt like I wasn't part of anything. I worked harder than I had ever worked. I felt like I was working in complete solitude – which I was, but with there being no phone/virtual calls it felt even more as if I were alone. It was worse when I heard what my friends were doing with their work – coffee catch ups, virtual team meetings, Zoom quizzes and things like that. But there was none of that for me. I suppose that's what made me realise how important that social contact is when I go to work and I won't take that for granted ever again. I've learnt that my work colleagues are as important as my friends because they are part of my life every day. I think lockdown has helped me see that a lot better and I appreciate the people I work with more. I also know now that I need to work with people who are a close group, who do spend time having virtual coffee mornings and regular team meetings and night time Zoom drinking sessions.

Being friendly and bubbly is so much part of me that I found it really hard to have that taken away by isolation and lockdown.

Lockdown happened and I was alone at work and alone at home – I can, hand on heart, say I've never felt so lonely in my life. I decided I needed to try and keep busy so I decided to paint all the garden fences, which kept me going for a while. But after that I fell deeper into depression and hardly left the house. My family were so worried about me that they made an appointment for me with the doctor and I was put on antidepressants.

Then I got a gorgeous wee kitten and he was the most adorable little thing. I had to take him at six weeks as his mum was feral. It was hard work feeding him every two hours but let me tell you, without a word of a lie, that this little creature saved my life! The love I had for him was unreal. He was the best thing I could have done for myself at that time too. He was my baby and he still is, nearly a year on. I felt like I had a purpose again. And even though he was just a tiny kitten I didn't feel so alone anymore.

After we came out of the first lockdown my son started coming to stay with me over the weekends and we grew closer than we ever had. It was really nice and I think that maybe him leaving gave us this new kind of relationship – more of an adult relationship or friendship than mother and child. I was starting to feel better, a combination of the antidepressants, the kitten and my son coming to stay regularly. When they announced the second lockdown my son asked if he could come back and stay at home with me. I nearly bit his hand off – of course it was okay! The second lockdown was completely different as I had my son and my kitten and, although things on the work front were still not good, I didn't feel as isolated or as depressed. We are now in lockdown three and although I still sometimes struggle with my depression it is nowhere near as bad as it was before when I didn't want to be here anymore. My relationships with my friends and family are so important to me and I am so thankful that my family knew me well enough to know how badly I was suffering and go to the doctor on my behalf because I don't think I'd have done it on my own. If I wasn't as close with them as I am I'd have had nobody looking out for me. Being single during lockdown is really hard; having no contact with another human is not normal, and especially for someone as sociable and outgoing as me.

It is really important if you feel depressed like I did that you ask for help. I honestly don't know what would've happened to me if I hadn't got the antidepressants from the doctor. I know it seems silly to say that a tiny kitten saved my life, but I do honestly think that's true. He gave me purpose, something to care for and kept me company when I was completely alone. He was soothing, helped calm me and he needed me. I needed him just as much. I had had a hard time before lockdown with my son leaving home and this meant I wasn't in a good place to start with. I think there are many, many other people out there who, like I was, were starting a rubbish time already at a really low point – I'm sure many of them were in situations way worse than I was too. I can only think how bad they must've felt because I really did feel that I couldn't go on anymore at times.

A SLOWER PACE OF LIFE

I had spent the winter of 2019/20 training for a half marathon, to be my first race at that distance for over three decades. As the day in mid-March 2020 approached it was becoming obvious that this strange, pneumonia-type virus that had been sweeping through parts of China and then Italy had arrived in Scotland. Things were developing so fast that the organisers seriously considered cancelling with just days to go. However, with suitable safety measures, the race went ahead and I was pleased to complete the distance. This was my first experience of social distancing: I loitered at the back of the field before the start, then 'allowed' the great mass of runners to disappear into the distance once the starter gun went off. That's what I told everyone anyway.

Just days later the pandemic restrictions – what we came to know as lockdown – were introduced. Initially I was quite relaxed about this as I thought it would be short term. In recent times outbreaks such as SARS, Swine Flu and Bird Flu, all serious diseases, had failed to develop into the new Spanish Flu type pandemic that we all feared. How mistaken I was.

Initially it was an adventure. Full disclosure: I am retired, so is my wife, and our two adult children both live and work at home. We were our own self-contained bubble and we certainly were not subject to the pressures experienced by working families with younger children. That said, I did have a number of health concerns – a leftover legacy of the days when

I didn't take care of myself as well as I should – so I knew I would have to be careful.

We were luckier than our friends in Italy and Spain, our lockdown wasn't as strict. There were restrictions but at least I could get outdoors for exercise. The thought also entered my head that my generation had not experienced anything more serious than a prolonged industrial dispute that turned out the lights or an oil crisis-fuelled period of inflation. We'd lived through no wars, famine, or even pandemics. So, at worst, during lockdown we were confined to our local area. I am a home-bird anyway; I love hanging around the house. Ask my wife, she sometimes has to literally drag me out.

The boredom soon set in, however. We had lived frugally and saved up for years in order to enjoy early retirement and now our plans were being frustrated. Our holiday to Lanzarote was cancelled just days before flying out, the camp sites across the country were closed so taking our campervan away was out, and we weren't even allowed to drive to the coast or countryside to enjoy a walk somewhere further afield. No social activity either. No seeing friends and family, no group training sessions with our running club, no organised races! It all started to get real.

Then the resilience, the self-reliance set in. After years of suffering from a depressive disorder I had had to learn coping skills. I had already learnt how to bounce back, how to put a positive slant on a situation (traits I later discovered I shared with others with similar, long-term conditions). Even this, which I was used to doing, became a challenge!

If I couldn't train with my running pals, well, running is essentially a solo activity, isn't it? The solitude gave me the opportunity to try out a technique that had always intrigued me: running slower to run faster. Running whilst keeping your pulse rate below your lactate threshold heart rate, essentially fuelling your activity by burning fat. It worked! I became faster because I was developing my aerobic fitness. It was also just so relaxing, an added bonus in this stressful time. By doing this I was keeping my body and my mind healthy.

Instead of races – which my wife and I normally do regularly – I took part in virtual challenges. Our running club and Scottish Athletics organised these: you had to run the required distance – say 5k – alone and on a route of your choosing, in your own locality, and then submit your time. I could maintain the friendly rivalries I had built up and still enjoy competitive running. Not only was I staying healthy but I was also connecting with people. Win-win!

Lockdown was also a time of introspection. A chance to look at what improvements I could make to my lifestyle. The initial panic-buying spree at the start of lockdown had scared me. I had long feared that the supermarket retail infrastructure, with its just-in-time ordering, was not as secure or as robust as it could be, and that seemed to be playing out as items disappeared from the shelves. I started to ration myself, cut down on my portions – and not just of toilet roll! – in order to make our stocks last. That led me to try and lose those last few pounds in weight that would take me to levels I had not seen for four decades. I'm not there yet, but I'm close, and I've almost got to the stage where I can come off my type II diabetes medication. That may have happened anyway, but lockdown definitely encouraged me to get healthier – a journey I had already started.

So many other good things happened as well and it's easy to forget them when things are difficult. We spent less on holidays, petrol and entertainment so we installed a new kitchen, fitted new carpets, bought new furniture. I decorated (I had the time!); not a good thing in itself but the finished results made it worthwhile. And the lack of traffic! I could run through the village during the day, down the middle of the normally busy trunk road, without getting splattered! It's the little things.

It hasn't been a perfect time but, and I know I am very fortunate in this, there were consolations. There were very real hardships, such as not being able to visit my wife's mum in her care home in northern England, but we're able to live at a slower pace and I have enjoyed completing my mazzles (map jigsaw puzzles) of mountains that I currently am not allowed to climb.

The main thing I've learnt from this period is how vulnerable we are, both individually and on a community level. Whatever remaining health vulnerabilities I had required careful management, and I have been successful in that. I've not had as much as a sniffle; is that because of the social distancing, the mask wearing, the increased attention to hygiene and cleanliness? And, for all our wealth and supposed organisation as a society, we really were not prepared for a crisis as deep as this.

I truly hope this period spurs us on to look at how we make the world a safer and more secure place to live. We have learnt, or should have done, that community health and community wealth affects us all. As earlier generations discovered, infectious diseases cannot be limited to areas of poverty. If people cannot isolate because they don't have the resources to do that properly then it's a problem – squalor and want for one is squalor and want for all.

IT'S RARE, BUT IT'S MEANT TO BE: A NEW RELATIONSHIP IN LOCKDOWN

It's rare, but every now and again you fall into a situation that is just meant to be. This instance is one of those times and we feel incredibly fortunate. We were both in a situation where we hadn't been in a relationship for quite some time, and as you can imagine feeling a bit, well… lonely. So lonely, in fact, that we both resorted to the one app we thought we would never use…yes, you guessed it – Tinder! When we spoke about it later and think back to what our friends said, we'd both been told that we *'wouldn't find a meaningful relationship'* on there and at the time, we both agreed.

Our first date was in a local pub on a cold evening toward the end of January 2020; maybe not the most romantic setting for our first date but one we both remember fondly. The connection was instant. We found numerous common interests and with the added fuel of copious amounts of alcohol, we continued to laugh until he had to get the last train home which we remember being a very sad affair. After that, we continued to chat and our relationship grew stronger. It wasn't long until he would drive up every night after work just to see me (a 60-mile round trip) and drive home the same night.

After only a few weeks, we were getting pretty serious. I had just started renting a one-bedroom flat which meant that our dates no longer had to be freezing walks to the lighthouse or sober nights in the pub (he had to drive). By this time, news of coronavirus was everywhere and lockdown loomed. Come March 2020, we had a decision to make: either he moved in with me after only knowing each other for a month or we would have to stay separated for however long the lockdown would last. To most, I assume that this would have been a really difficult decision committing to living with a partner you have only known for a month but for us, it was simple. The thought of not seeing each other for more than a week was too much and we decided to go for it and we moved in together.

As soon as lockdown hit, I was furloughed and he was unable to work as a freelance photographer. This was, of course, by far the most time we had spent together. It was perfect. We really got to know each other and had no external interruptions. It could've gone the other way so we realise how lucky we are to have found each other and to have found each other at the right time.

We started planning a road trip through Oban along the coast through Fort William and stopping off at his hometown Grantown-on-Spey. It would be the first time we had been away together and we both knew that we had exciting times ahead, especially since we had been in lockdown for so long. Although lockdown was still in place when we planned our trip, we did it in the hope that lockdown restrictions would be lifted by the time it came around. We bought all of the essentials needed including a tent and some camping furniture.

We decided to try out our camping gear to celebrate a milestone in our relationship in style, even though it wasn't anywhere far away or glamorous because of lockdown. We pitched our newly bought tent and draped fairy lights around the poles. We bought delicious food and sat about having a wee drink and a lot of fun. We did not, however, know this would be the only time that the tent got out. On the Friday before our holiday was due to commence, my work called to say they would like me back to work on the Monday - road trip cancelled. We were both gutted, but at the same time financially we were relieved.

It was a relief going back to work considering the circumstances with the job market at the time. However, I don't think either of us realised how hard it was going to be for me to go from being with someone 24/7 to those hours I spent at work away from him. I think this made me realise how special our relationship was and how I knew it was meant to be, as cheesy as that sounds. We're both still young – in our early twenties – but lockdown has made this relationship so strong that we can't see our lives being any other way.

We felt so lucky that we had each other during the strict lockdown and we both agree that if he hadn't moved in, our relationship wouldn't be half as strong as it is now. It cut my bills in half, which is also a bonus! I think this past year has made us realise more than ever that life can throw pretty hard punches but if you have someone by your side that you really care about, it just feels like a pillow, a big duck down fluffy pillow.

THE DARKNESS MOVES IN

My phone captures so much of my life. It's full of photos and videos of our adventures as a family, and it holds most of the day-to-day interactions I have with family, friends and colleagues. Because of this, when I was asked to reflect upon what it had been like to live during a global pandemic I automatically reached for my phone to remind myself exactly what life had been like. What struck me was that while my phone was largely full of images that captured love, laughter and joy, there were very few images that captured the more visceral emotions of anger, sorrow and despair. These were hinted at, often through jokes, but they were never fully spoken of. It's like looking at a metaphorical black hole; the absence of that inner and more private turmoil is so stark.

The old 'normal' that's captured in my phone is full of vibrant colours. There're the bright colours in Gran Canaria that we visited with my parents and three-year-old son around the time that the first case of the SARS-CoV-2 virus was recorded. At the end of 2019 there are the pictures of family coming together at Christmas to go to the pantomime, eat good food and exchange presents around the tree. At Hogmanay there are pictures of the Chinese Lantern display. There are the bright colours of my parents' kitchen on New Year's Day as we gathered as a family for my mum's birthday and my dad's annual buffet dinner. January and February pass by in images of my son and his friends at their pre-school Spanish class.

There are the bright colours and smiles of children's birthday parties. The laughter of cousins playing together. There are the messages about planned sleepovers and family meals. The photos are vibrant and loud, and the only thing that they fail to capture is the more mundane aspects of slotting our socialising into 'life'.

What *is* absent from my phone, however, are a lot of the images that I viewed on its screen during the first few months of 2020. Those photos were taken by strangers in places far away, and their dull, muted and dark colours contrast sharply with the vibrant images of my life at that time. Those photos contain the industrial greys and browns of China that began to appear on our TV's. They're the empty grey and brown cobble streets of Italy after their lockdown. They're the images of drab green army trucks transporting coffins of COVID-19 victims after the cemeteries and crematoriums in Bergamo were unable to keep pace with the rate at which people were dying. They're of field hospitals being constructed around the world by the military. They're the satellite images of thousands of graves dug in the brown earth of Iran. These are not images that evoke joy, peace or tranquillity. They're images that evoke an overwhelming sense of anxiety and despair. They're the images that kept you awake at night.

In my mind the slide show of washed out colours continues. There's the dull pink prescription sheet for antibiotics and the dull red of my steroid inhaler when I couldn't stop coughing after sharing an office with someone who'd been skiing in Northern Italy. There's the greyness of empty shelves as people panic bought soap, toilet roll and food. There are the dull colours of the modelling charts which concluded that critical care capacity in the UK would be completely overwhelmed and that up to quarter of a million people could die if social distancing was not put in place immediately. And there's the huddled black mass of bodies crowded together in a football stadium after the UK government chose to ignore the evidence and pursue an idiotic plan for herd immunity instead. There's the memory of the colourless glass of gin and tonic that I poured as I realised back in March 2020 that what was being modelled was repeated cycles of lockdowns that would be triggered and eased by ICU bed capacity until a vaccine was successfully created and rolled out; and I knew that given the challenges of vaccine creation and distribution we could be living this way for two years, perhaps longer. But perhaps most vivid is the hideous green couch and the ugly salmon walls behind the Prime Minister as he announced that *from this evening…you must stay home'*. It seems fitting that these joyless colours are associated with the UK closing its doors and of life as we knew it slipping away. They're colours I won't forget. They're colours I now hate.

But life didn't slip away. It just changed. It became more challenging and complex. The images in my phone reflect the extra time I got to spend with my son and the adventures we had. The images are still vibrant and colourful. They hold the memories of my son sitting inside the multi-coloured car that we built out of cardboard boxes during our first 14-day period of self-isolation after a fever that lasted all of six hours. There are the bright colours of the rainbow that we painted on our living room window for children to see on their daily walks. There is the bright red of my son's bike in the living room after we converted it into an exercise bike by placing its stabilisers into a pair of running shoes. There are images of baking and science experiments. There's picture after picture that include the bright blue skies of spring as we played in the garden for hours on end because the rules said we could leave our home once a day for exercise and there was no way in hell that we were going back inside until it was dark. There are pictures of us transforming the communal gardens from drab spaces to ones filled with colourful plants and food grown from seed. Those images capture the fun times of being asked to stay at home in order to stay safe, save lives and protect our beloved NHS.

But they do not tell the whole story. They're the colours of the fun times. The colours of the times when work didn't intrude into our home and cause tension, resentment and disconnection. They're not the harsh glowing blue of a laptop screen in a dark room at seven o'clock in the morning as you try to get some work done before you have to try to be both mum and employee simultaneously. They're not the golden amber colour of yet another glass of wine poured of an evening because you are hurting and the nice, warm fuzzy feeling of the alcohol makes you forget for a while. They're not the caramel colour of your bedroom walls; a colour that you used to love but now despise because you work in the same room that you sleep in because you don't want the tales of child abuse and neglect that live in your computer intruding on the happy spaces of your home. They're not the dark shadows of your room when you can't sleep because of the anxiety and fear. They're not the dull greyish colour that resides in eyes that used to sparkle blue when you looked in the mirror. Or the dullness of hair that you no longer wash unless you have a video call. No. These are the colours that your camera chooses not to capture. They're the feelings that message chats with friends and colleagues allude to, but only in jest.

And *still* these are not the bad times. The bad times don't have colour as everything bright just fades to black. The black times are the absolute feellngs of rage when your husband's work won't acknowledge that there are two adults trying to work from home because they think that he shouldn't be doing childcare when he has a wife who can look after his child. They're the times when that anger and frustration spills out and the adults in the house are shouting at each other while the three-year-old tries not to hear and then that awful sadness that he did. They're that time when your son refuses to talk to his grandparents for weeks on end because he's feeling rejected and hurt so he's pushed them away. They're the days when your son is physically attacking your husband because he's decided that daddy is to blame for lockdown because he keeps saying *'no, we're not allowed to do that'*. They're the times when you find your son biting his wrists to stop himself from crying because *'I can't cry mummy'* and you wonder if the reason he can't cry is because if he starts he will never stop? You understand that. You feel the same way.

The black times are the times when you just sit and stare at the wall because nobody taught you how to parent an emotionally distressed toddler, and the hug from his grandparents that will ease his pain is forbidden by law. It's the day that you sit in your garden in the sunshine and cry because the father of a former colleague is one of the nearly 800 people who died from COVID-19 the previous day. They're the times when you feel absolute rage as you think about how the UK government chose to ignore the science and instead implemented policies that have resulted in the highest rate of mortality in the world and one of the worst economic fallouts. They're that time when you stand sobbing in your kitchen because your ten-year-old niece's first experience of a funeral was standing at the side of the road and watching a priest bless the coffin of her next-door neighbour as it sat inside the hearse. The black times are all of those times when it all just got too much and you didn't know how you were ever going to survive. And when those black times came you soon learned that the only thing you *could* do to ride them out was to open the window, lean out and gulp deep shaking breaths of fresh air to try and let nature soothe you.

As we emerged from the safety of our home and garden into the 'new normal' it was those blue and green hues of spring and summer that slowly began to repair the damage that lockdown had done to my soul. As I re-joined society I found myself appreciating all the little things that I once took for granted. Things like the joy of wandering through the aisles of a garden centre to buy new plants for our garden, and then sitting on the grass outside to eat strawberry shortcakes we purchased on a whim. Of standing by the banks of a loch on a grey overcast day skipping stones. Of just living in the moment and not taking life for granted. And when we were allowed to visit family again, I know I will forever treasure that image of my son wearing a Spiderman facemask and a bright blue puddle suit that had been bleached so that he could sneak an illegal cuddle with his grandparents on Father's Day; a cuddle that I allowed because I knew that those hugs were the only thing that would truly erase the sadness that had taken hold of his heart. I revelled in the sounds of the excited squeals, laughter and tears that accompanied those cuddles, even while every cell in me screamed with envy that I wanted a hug too! I wish I could feel sorry for this breach of the regulations, but as I watched my son sit and animatedly talk to my parents for the first time in nearly three months I couldn't feel guilty. His mental health mattered more.

Those memories of reconnection are splashed with colour. There's the bright green of the playing fields that the children played on as I talked to my parents and brother in the sunshine. There's the blue of the River Clyde as we sat on the seafront eating ice cream. There's the yellow, turquoise, navy and pink of the camping chairs that we would spend the next few months sitting on in my parent's garden as we laughed and talked. There's the orange and black of the butterflies that we raised from caterpillars during lockdown and released into the wild. They're the colours of our rebirth into life. A vibrant, wonderful, colourful life that had been tainted by the dark storm of the pandemic.

But, as vibrant as that life was, it still felt strange as your 'new normal' was a facsimile of the life that you used to have due to the ever-changing list of restrictions that controlled everything you did. And it was those restrictions, that abnormality, within each of the activities that reminded you that things weren't 'normal'. That abnormality was present in the way that you chose to go to busy adventure parks in the pouring rain because you knew few other people would be crazy enough and you wouldn't have to worry about whether other people were keeping their distance or using sanitizer. It was present the day you had to talk yourself out of a panic attack as your son rode a fairground ride at the zoo because your brain couldn't reconcile the fact that you were out having fun while thousands upon thousands of people were dying; and it was present as you vowed to yourself that if you couldn't control the anxiety with breathing exercises and behavioural techniques that you'd take medication to keep life feeling as normal as possible for your child. It was present all those times you couldn't breathe in the supermarket because there were just too many damned people. It was present in the feeling of guilt that you had when you complained about how awful your own experiences of lockdown had been when you knew that there were people who had had a much worse time. And it was present in the crazy reality of having to read multiple sets of government guidelines in order to plan any activity, and then having to read another set of guidelines when the rules changed two weeks later. It was draining. But the abnormal was as 'normal' as it was going to get and it was just a case of giving into it, trying to adapt and go with the flow.

By the time July 2020 arrived we'd begun to adapt. Our mornings were dull and sleepy. I sat on the bed and worked while my son watched TV and complained that he was bored. But as soon as the computer was closed and we'd had lunch, we would leave my husband working and take off for the outside world. Our afternoons became a blur of activities: picnics in the park with friends and colleagues, barbeques and marshmallow roasting with friends; riverside walks; walks on the beach, collecting seashells and skimming stones; paddling in the sea; walking alpacas; visiting zoos and safari parks; harvesting fruit and vegetables; and sharing my child's love of trainspotting. It was a life that was full of routine and bursting at the seams. But it was a life seriously lacking in physical interaction and connection. And the wide-angle shots in my phone capture the distance between our friends and family. We were together, but it was a together that was apart. And it was lonely, even though it made us laugh and smile.

The absence of physical interaction was softened by the Scottish Government announcement that children under the age of twelve no longer needed to socially distance from adults. If I'm honest I don't think that even discovering that I was pregnant all those years ago held as much joy as being able to shout *'Nicola says you can have hugs'* to my son and his wee cousin, and watching their faces break out into huge grins before they raced to each other with open arms. Many tears were shed that day, all tears of joy. My nephew's pudgy little arms wrapped around my neck was bliss. And that feeling of pure joy was repeated with cuddles from my niece the next day. And although it hurt that we still weren't allowed to hug parents and siblings, I soon discovered that being able to smell the reassuring and familiar scent of my dad on my son as we snuggled at the end of the day made life that little bit more bearable. It wasn't a hug, but my brain remembered being enveloped in the safety, love and comfort of that smell. It remembered what that smell meant. It meant love. It meant home. And my soul felt lighter.

But there were times in those summer months when the darkness crept back in. The most notable related to the road trip to England. In the weeks before we were due to travel the infection rates started to slowly creep up in the North of England and Westminster announced a series of local lockdowns. The rise in cases was mainly confined to the North West, but there were a few areas in Yorkshire that were included and I found myself browsing the small area infection statistics on a regular basis so that I could make an informed decision about whether or not it was safe to travel as I'd decided we'd only go if the infection rate where we were going was lower than ours (amongst other things). It was complicated; I'd never done this before and the libraries were closed so I couldn't get a copy of the *'Dummy's Guide to Planning a Vacation During a Global Pandemic'*. I had already booked some activities prior to the lockdowns being announced so another fun evening activity became cross checking the postcodes of those activities against those contained within the lockdown boundaries to make sure that we'd not be entering a lockdown area per Scottish Government guidance not to travel to those areas. English and Scottish regulations differed quite significantly, and certain English regulations for children triggered feelings of immense anger that the needs and rights of children in England had been pushed aside in favour of allowing adults to dine out and go to the pub. It all seemed completely at odds with the life that we had been living over the last couple of months. After reading the English guidance and getting annoyed I decided that, in most cases, it would be simpler to adhere to Scottish guidance as they seemed much safer.

The day before we were due to travel my mum phoned to inform us that she was on her way to Glasgow Airport for a test as she had developed a cough. My blood ran cold. If the test came back positive we would have to isolate as we had been in her house the day before. I wasn't really worried about our trip, it could be rearranged. I was worried about my mum.

And I was worried that we would have to spend another long, tedious 14 days inside if she tested positive. I didn't sleep much that night. At 7am my phone beeped – she'd tested negative! Thank God. I checked the infection rates and they were lower than ours so we packed and headed off on our adventures, leaving Daddy at home to work in peace.

Our first stop was East Links Family Park just outside of North Berwick. It was a great day, but throughout it I felt quite unsettled by the actions of one large group of British-Asian visitors and I spent a lot of our time at the park deliberately choosing activities that kept us away from where they were congregating because they were not socially distancing and the composition of their groups kept changing. I watched them interact and was horrified when they all came together and boarded the train as one party of 40 people! Now that I was looking at them more closely it appeared that there were at least four generations of the same family and it was actually mind-boggling watching how they were behaving. The researcher in me couldn't help but wonder about how public health messaging was being tailored for minority groups given that this group didn't seem to have a clue that there was even a global pandemic and I was aware of the significantly higher rate of mortality among the black, Asian and minority ethnic populations. There was clearly something seriously wrong with the message the UK government was portraying to minority groups.

That unsettled feeling remained as we drove south down the A1 and encountered overhead gantry after overhead gantry stating that local travel restrictions applied within England. Despite knowing that where we were going was not subject to restrictions I found myself reflecting on the fact that I'd never before felt scared or uneasy about crossing the border into England. It was a strange feeling. The feeling of uneasiness returned as we approached Yorkshire and we saw sign after sign advising of local lockdowns and telling us that only essential travel was permitted. I hadn't realised we'd have to drive through some of the towns subject to lockdown measures to get to where we were going. I looked at the petrol gauge and was thankful that we wouldn't have to stop anywhere. Walking through the corridors of our hotel it seemed like we were the only ones adhering to the signs requesting that masks be worn in public areas. Mask usage also seemed so much poorer in shops than at home. And there were several times that I cringed when I heard the words 'optional' in conjunction with 'track and trace'; everywhere I had been at home there was no 'optional', just a request for a telephone number that nobody seemed to bat an eyelid at. It was all very different from my experiences at home, and it made me wonder how the public health messaging was going so wrong down in England. All this aside, our trip was amazing. It was so much fun; but despite the fun I was relieved to get home as it genuinely felt much safer in Scotland. And the statistics agreed as Scotland was slowly heading towards achieving zero COVID status; an amazing feat and something that it felt like we could be really proud of after four long months of restrictions.

As nurseries returned and we continued to be allowed to visit people overnight in their homes the darkness lifted further. We smiled more. We laughed more. And the few remaining behavioural difficulties my son had been displaying disappeared completely. We continued our adventures in the afternoons, but now my son also chatted happily about all of the fun things he'd got to do with his friends and his grandparents while we worked. With my son in nursery I moved the laptop with its stories of child abuse out of my bedroom and into the sitting room. That simple act of my child being cared for by somebody else proved enough to provide the separation between work and home again. My days were no longer spent surrounded by caramel walls but light colours and family photos. I started to consume far less alcohol than I did during lockdown as the boredom and isolation lifted. Despite the fact that life was still abnormal, it was starting to feel bearable.

As the leaves turned into a sea of reds, oranges, purples and golds our life began to change again. My son was delighted as gymnastics, football, rugby, swimming and athletics returned. He surprised me by adapting quickly to my being unable to sit and watch as he did gymnastics, and we quickly fell into the routine of him lining up at the door and walking in as I went back to my car or to the gym. I resumed swimming. It felt great to have all of these little slices of normality back.

And yet the darkness still tried to intrude. There was the morning I arrived at the swimming pool and discovered that a mobile testing centre had been set up outside, and my inner voice screamed *fuck off* at this unwelcome intruder into the relaxing time I'd carved out for myself. There was the day we arrived at my son's gymnastic class and discovered that the way that the children entered and exited the class had been changed because a flu vaccination clinic had been set up inside the same hall. There was the realisation that the diary in your phone looked so busy because you had been religiously capturing everywhere that you and your family had been, when and with whom, in case you needed that information for contact tracers. And then there was the steady stream of cars that arrived at the testing centre outside of the leisure centre where your son did his classes; something that you religiously tried to ignore but couldn't as the tests were happening less than twenty metres away from where you were sat. These things were all unwelcome reminders that the full life you were living was subject to threat and could be taken away again very easily. It was these things that disturbed your sleep and left you exhausted.

As the colourful leaves of autumn started to fall from the trees and turn to dark, decomposing mulch on the floor the hard-won freedoms of summer also died one by one. Household visits were banned in mid-September, but fortunately childcare exemptions were made for key workers and I felt thankful for the fact that as a category two worker my son could continue to be cared for by his grandparents. His being allowed to go into my parents' house while I was not allowed did cause some problems as they looked after him two days a week and we usually slept over at their house because of the distance from home. I talked to my son about sleeping over without mummy and he started to cry. We lived an hour away so if he wasn't willing to sleepover by himself then I would have to drive four hours a day to take him, return home to work and then collect him again. The thought of driving that much was not appealing so I booked a hotel nearby; this wasn't the great solution that I thought it would be as I couldn't access the secure network that all my work was hosted on because of the hotel Wi-Fi. There was also the small, minor issue that I couldn't check-in to my room until after noon. So, when it was dry I worked in my parents' garden wrapped up in warm clothes and blankets, fingerless gloves keeping my hands warm as I typed. When it was wet I worked in my car until I could get in my hotel room.

As September went on the infection rates continued to rise and the threat level was increased by the Chief Medical Officers of the UK. In Scotland we were told to reduce the number of daily contacts we had. I experienced my first COVID test after something caused my asthma to go into overdrive and I found myself coughing more frequently than normal. I suspected it was just the changing seasons and playing outdoors among the autumn leaves, but it needed to be checked. I tested negative. My son cheered and hugged me as I told him that he no longer had to isolate. Later that week we went glamping at Loch Tay. We stayed in a pod, played in the woods, paddled in the loch and generally just recharged our batteries. On a night time we searched for constellations and planets and toasted marshmallows. I didn't want to go home. My husband agreed. He hadn't left our house overnight since December 2019 and hadn't realised just how much he was sick of the four walls.

The changes in restrictions and increasing levels of infection meant we had to review all of the plans that we'd made for my son's fourth birthday. Around the time of the restrictions first being eased at the end of May I had read a document by the Scottish Government that had included a modelling forecast that suggested that restrictions would likely be reintroduced mid-October. I had enough statistics training to understand the potential limits of the epidemiological models being produced so rather than accepting them carte-blanche I decided to plan several activities for my son's birthday in the hope that we would be able to do just one fun thing. We planned a small party. The plan was that the children would get to do animal handling and then we would spend the afternoon playing in the woods come rain or shine. But I'd planned the party when adults from four households were allowed to gather and that was no longer permitted. I spent that evening reading the guidance on regulated and unregulated children's activities and talking to the owner of the petting zoo. Her understanding of the guidance was that they could run the event with a maximum of ten children but adults were not permitted to stay. I presented all of this information to the other parents who agreed that they were happy to go ahead. We'd still play in the woods afterwards but the parents would have to choose a buddy to hang out with so we were sticking to the two-household rule. We laughed at the absurdity of it all.

The week of his birthday rolled around. Somehow luck was in his favour so everything we planned went ahead but on party day a storm was forecast. Typical. It was wet and windy but it looked like the worst wouldn't hit until the evening. The children sat in their wet weather gear and took turns meeting and holding animals and doing other activities. We were all absolutely soaked, but nobody cared. As crazy as it all was I thought to myself that this might actually be my favourite day of 2020. Nobody in their right minds would even consider holding a party like this in October if it wasn't for coronavirus. It made me realise we try to protect our children from the elements too much. What's the saying? *There is no such thing as bad weather, just inappropriate clothing*. It's true. The children had a blast. Before we all left, one of the children said *that party was awesome*. It had been awesome.

The re-imposition of restrictions came just two days later. Curfews were imposed on hospitality and all licensed premises within the central belt of Scotland were to close. We'd probably have to start queuing outside of shops again. Oh joy. After months of adjusting to our new colourful life the darkness returned. As the weather deteriorated and the days got darker, my parents suggested that we should form an official childcare bubble to make life easier and I would live with them on the days I required childcare. I agonised over their suggestion for days; having worked in public health research for 13 years I had more than a passing interest in public health policy and, as the Swiss Health Minister bluntly put it earlier in the year: *it is not the grandchildren that will kill their grandparents, it will be their own children*. If anybody was going to infect my parents it'd be me, and I didn't know how I'd live with myself if that happened.

I told them no. My mum pointed out that their house was on three stories and the entire top floor could be isolated from the rest of the house as it had a separate bathroom. If I purchased a small fridge to store food and drinks I could isolate myself for the entire time. I still felt torn, but it was a pragmatic solution and if I also wore masks when moving through the communal areas of their house and didn't interact with them unless I was outdoors then the risk would actually be fairly small. We agreed that we would all isolate if either of our households got symptoms and I said yes. I spoke to my parents' neighbours about what I was doing and showed them my key worker letter. And from the middle of October I started sleeping over at my parents' house again while they watched my son. I still didn't like it. And the resurgence of insomnia, the more frequent headaches and general feeling of malaise I felt while there suggested that my body agreed. I found myself having lots of morbid thoughts in the middle of the night about my parents being dead when we woke. The first night I stayed I shared a glass of wine with my mum via Zoom. It was possibly the most ridiculous and tragic thing that I've ever done, and I never did it again as it hurt too much to be trapped upstairs alone. During the day I heard my parents and son laughing and talking while I worked. It was lovely to hear, but it made me feel very alone. As the weeks ticked by I realised that I'd gone from not really drinking over the summer to drinking one to two glasses of wine most nights.

The darkness continued to grow. The numbers of cars arriving at the testing centre while I was waiting for my son steadily increased. I tried not to watch, but it was hard to ignore. Friends and acquaintances who worked in COVID wards during the first wave started telling me that they didn't know how they were going to survive the winter. A friend who worked in A&E told me that it was hell already and she felt like quitting (she didn't). Another friend who worked as an occupational therapist told me that their wards were filling up far too fast with COVID patients. I worried about their mental health, and how the health service would function in the future as the trauma their staff experienced finally started to take its toll. Slowly more and more people we knew disclosed that they or their family members and friends had tested positive for the virus. It felt like it was worse this time around, even though I logically knew that it was probably just that with the increased testing we were simply more aware of the virus' presence than we had been back at the start. Over the coming weeks I noticed that the number of ambulances on the road was increasing. It felt scary again.

As Halloween approached it was like living with an overwhelming sense of déjà vu. We were living life to the fullest we could while waiting for the announcement that would once again flip our lives upside down. We went pumpkin picking with my son's friends. The next day we took my son to the safari park for more Halloween fun. The photos of those days are so warm and colourful, and over the next few months I discovered that when the darkness became too much just looking at them helped to chase black thoughts away.

Two days after our pumpkin picking trip my son developed a temperature and cough. I phoned my parents to tell them to quarantine and then booked him his first COVID test. He was scared and begged me not to take him. I felt really mean as I explained that he could have a test *or* he could stay inside for fourteen days as neither option was fun. He grudgingly agreed that he would go if I was tested too. Tests booked, we headed to the airport, my little one crying in the back of the car. He helped me complete my test, holding my wrist as I swirled the cotton swab inside my nose and then across my tonsils for the requisite 15 seconds and then sat quietly on my lap as I swabbed his nostrils. As I watched the older child in the car next to us sobbing hysterically and pleading with his mum not to swab his throat I was glad that because my son was under the age of five I only had to swab his nostrils as having to do his tonsils would've been impossible. On the way home, I messaged the parents of the children we'd been pumpkin picking with to let them know what was happening and warn them that if the test came back positive they'd have to isolate. Fortunately, the tests came back negative.

The new levels system introduced in Scotland in October didn't really affect us much as I required informal childcare; my son could still go to nursery and we could travel for his sports and swimming. There was one thing that proved to completely undo my son though, and that was no trick or treating. Telling him that nobody was allowed to trick or treat was awful. As we sat on the floor he buried his head into my neck and asked *'why is Nicola Sturgeon so mean?'*. I had to explain to him that Nicola wasn't mean and that she was doing a really good job to keep all of us safe which meant she had to ask people not to do things. I told him that if we asked Nicola about all of this she'd tell us that she hated coronavirus as much as we did. Then the Prime Minister announced that England would be going back into lockdown as their virus rates were spiralling out of control. As friends living in England messaged to convey their frustration and despair, I just hoped that the levels system that had been announced in Scotland – along with restrictions implemented when the virus had been circulating at lower levels – would be enough to prevent us from having to follow suit as the idea of having to adhere to another 'stay at home' order was mentally unbearable.

November arrived and we ended up back in isolation after my dad developed a temperature and cough. As my parents headed to the airport to be tested I tried to prepare my son for the possibility that we could be at my parents' house for the next few weeks depending upon the results. I spent my time trying to hide my foul mood from my son; the idea of having to spend up to 21 days in my little prison upstairs had made me want to scream. Thankfully his test was negative. The rest of November was a bit of an emotional rollercoaster if I'm honest. Biden won the US Presidential Election and we cried tears of joy, danced in the living room and drank champagne at four o'clock in the afternoon to celebrate the reign of the lunatic Trump being over. Pfizer BioNTech published their vaccine trial results demonstrating that they'd produced a vaccine with efficacy rates that were way beyond anything that anybody could've ever hoped for and there was finally a glimmer of hope that this mess could come to an end within the next year. But although there was hope there was also uncertainty. My curiosity as a researcher meant that I tended to look in detail at the infection data and it'd been two weeks since the lockdown in England had begun and there was still no indication in the data that the lockdown was working. I didn't understand why. I began to worry that something was going on that we didn't know about. That worry increased more when my boss told me that family living in the South of England were advising her to cancel her planned trip at Christmas as things were getting really bad down there. Something was wrong. I didn't know what, but if it was anything like it had been in March it would slowly sweep through the country over the next few weeks. I quietly started arranging a few Christmas activities for us to do during November; just in case we were prohibited from doing anything in December. My husband told me I was insane. I told him to shut up: we were doing Christmas activities in November!

So, in the middle of November we went to feed Santa's reindeer much to my sister-in-law's amusement and my husband's dismay. The next day I discovered that a local garden centre had just opened their Christmas section. So mid-November we put our Christmas jumpers on, put Christmas songs on in the car and headed off for an afternoon of festive fun. The next day Moderna announced that their vaccine worked, and we continued our attempts to feel festive by making decorations for our Christmas tree. Then my attempt to spread festive cheer backfired spectacularly. Having watched Glasgow's Christmas lights being switched on online my son asked if we could drive through Glasgow and see the lights. It was nine o'clock at night as we drove into the city; the streets were deserted and we wandered around George Square looking at the lights and the large Christmas tree. It made me feel absolutely wretched. All I could see was how cold and empty it was and it contrasted so sharply with the warm, happy memories of Christmases past that were rushing through my mind. I took a picture of him smiling in front of the Christmas tree that was usually surrounded by people. That was what was missing. People. People Make Glasgow. It really didn't feel like Glasgow without the people. That night I lay in bed and cried. It all felt so hopeless, and the next day that feeling continued as my area was put into level four restrictions. No swimming. No rugby. No gymnastics. No athletics. There was just work and nursery. And although I knew that my son would still be allowed to see my parents for childcare, it didn't change how lonely it felt to sit in my brother's old bedroom while he played downstairs. I didn't know how much more of this I could take.

During that period of feeling sorry for myself the UK and Scottish Governments announced that we'd be allowed to have Christmas with our families. Apparently three households would be allowed to form a 'Christmas Bauble' for five days and travel between the four home nations to do so. On the one hand I was happy at the news as I really wanted my son to have a 'normal' Christmas, but on the other hand I thought it was the most insanely dangerous idea I'd ever heard. I honestly didn't know how anybody in their right mind could seriously suggest a plan like this when across the UK there were around 500 people dying every day from COVID-19. Was being able to sit around the dinner table with our families really worth the risk? I felt like screaming as friends working in the NHS messaged to say that the announcement terrified them. I felt like screaming even more when it was announced that England were easing their lockdown! Their numbers were far too high to be exiting lockdown; and members of SAGE disclosed one by one that they had recommended the exact opposite, but once again Boris Johnson and his merry band of clowns knew better than the scientists. It infuriated me that we were now nearly nine months into restrictions and Westminster were still refusing to listen to what the evidence was telling them. Even the news that the Pfizer BioNTech vaccine had been given emergency authorisation for use by the MHRA couldn't lift the red curtain of rage that I felt.

As I silently raged at the incompetence of Westminster I discovered that my brother and parents were self-isolating because somebody in his work had decided to go into work while she was awaiting the results of a COVID-19 test! She'd tested positive, and through her own stupidity and selfishness she'd already managed to infect one other person who my brother had been working with in the last 24 hours. Unfortunately, he was informed of his need to isolate by the NHS an hour after he'd gone out for dinner with my parents. By the time they finished telling me all this I was actually shaking with rage at the stupidity of this woman. I couldn't understand how she could've been so stupid. I could've understood it, even had sympathy for her actions, if she'd turned into work because she was worried about losing income. But she wasn't: she was a salaried council employee who didn't have to worry about losing pay. I felt like screaming. I didn't think the risk was high that any of them had been infected, but it was difficult not to worry. My parents decided that they were going to isolate out of caution and, although their choice meant that I lost my childcare for two weeks, I was glad because had they looked after my son and then developed symptoms it would have meant that he'd have had to spend Christmas in isolation. The news that the AstraZeneca vaccine had been found to be effective passed by barely noticed.

The emotional rollercoaster continued throughout December. My phone beeped repeatedly with messages from friends in the NHS who'd received their appointments for COVID vaccinations. Each one of those messages made me smile. And they were not just little smiles, but huge cheesy grins. That joy soon dissipated when my son cuddled into me on the couch and whispered that he was worried that Santa wouldn't be able to come because of the travel restrictions. I reassured him that Santa Claus would be coming, and told him that because he was a key worker Nicola had said that he was going to be one of the first people to get the vaccine so he'd be safe. I later found out that this whole episode had made my mum completely break down in tears at the absolute injustice of a four-year-old being scared of Santa not coming to his house. I worried about children up and down the country who shared the same concerns, which led to me worrying about all of the children whose parents wouldn't be able to afford presents or food due to the financial burdens of the pandemic. That afternoon we decided to participate in five random acts of kindness, and we let our son choose charities to donate money, food and toys to.

Despite the restrictions we did enjoy lots of Christmas cheer: online streamed pantomimes; Christmas parties on Zoom; we watched the CBeebies Christmas Panto; we watched Santa cycle around a nearby town; we watched the Funbox Christmas special online; and we searched for Santa in the woods with my nephew. I even found myself being pleasantly surprised at just how enjoyable the staff Christmas party on Zoom proved to be as we all sat in our living rooms in

Christmas jumpers, eating snacks, drinking our tipple of choice and playing silly games.

Trying to have fun in the weeks leading up to Christmas wasn't without frustration though as all of the guidance around what we could and couldn't do was difficult to decipher as general guidance and Christmas guidance were often contradictory. It all seemed mad and I was completely confused! Basically, the guidance stated that I could go drive to a garden centre a few miles outside of our local boundary where I'd booked an outdoor visit to Santa, park and walk around outside, but I couldn't take my child to go and actually *see* Santa Claus who was also going to be outside. It was absolute nonsense, and I was relieved to discover that I was not alone as parent after parent expressed the same confusion online. Yes, I knew that the rules were basically there to stop us doing something stupid like travelling too far, and I'd already cancelled all of the trips that involved us travelling any distance, but this just seemed nonsensical. We saw Santa.

A week before Christmas the festive buzz was at complete odds with the harsh reality of the statistics. A new strain of COVID-19 had been identified and it was estimated to be 70% more transmissible than the strain we'd been living with all year. Between the new variant and the idiotic decision to relax England's lockdown at the start of December the UK now had around 6,000 more cases of COVID-19 being reported per day than when the English lockdown had been announced at Halloween. *'Oh well, at least everyone got to do their Christmas shopping and everybody in the UK got to have an amazing Christmas full of fun!'* What's that? *'Christmas is cancelled for everyone in the South East of England and London and everybody else is no longer getting the five days with their family that they had been promised?'.* Oh, and because the new strain had been allowed to spiral out of control in England, the Scottish Government had decided to place all of mainland Scotland into lockdown on Boxing Day. Now, I know the new variant really taking hold just at the point that vaccines started to be administered was really bad luck, but can I just request that if we are ever unlucky enough to have to live through a global pandemic again that nobody does anything as monumentally stupid as promising people that they can spend five days with their loved ones? Providing people with that level of false hope was just cruel.

With the Boxing Day lockdown announcement our plans to see our in-laws went out the window so we quickly arranged lunch for the next day. We had a lovely time; it wasn't the post-Christmas get together that we'd planned but it was lovely. While plans with the in-laws were hastily rearranged, Christmas with my parents wasn't really affected by the changes announced as my plan had always been that we would just remain at the house on Christmas Eve after my work rather than driving home, and my husband would join us so that we could spend Christmas Day together. After putting an excited wee boy to bed on Christmas Eve I went down to the living room wearing a mask – I was not sitting upstairs by myself on Christmas Eve! I opened the window, found a spot on the floor around two metres away from my parents and we sat talking over a bottle of wine. This proved dangerous and before long we were quite merrily drunk; I was still two metres away but the mask was now sat on the floor as 'drunk me' could no longer be bothered taking it on and off between drinks. A little voice in my head kept telling me that we shouldn't be doing this, it was too risky; my heart told my head to shut up and fuck off. I quietly tried to reassure the anxious voice in my head that we'd had minimal social contacts in the last seven days and as we'd be in an enforced lockdown from Boxing Day the risks to others was low. The only risk right now was to us and we were all consenting adults who'd been living in an unofficial bubble for months. The only difference between tonight and all of those weeks before was that I felt happy rather than sad. I felt connected, not alone. My husband appeared just after 1am; his appearance made us laugh as he'd followed the rules and travelled to join us on Christmas Day. We opened another bottle of wine and the next day we woke up with sore heads. Christmas Day was fun. My little one revelled in having us all in the same place. The windows were open and we tried to maintain our distance as much as possible, but after a night sitting unmasked talking we abandoned the masks because if any of us were infected the damage had already been done. My dad cooked dinner.

As the day went on it became apparent that my dad wasn't well. It turned out that while I was sat upstairs isolated in that little room I'd missed the fact that he hadn't been well for a while. I asked my mum what was going on and she told me that he'd had a really sore back for weeks, but was refusing to go to the doctors because he said it was because he wasn't walking enough because he was furloughed. Standing in the kitchen talking to him later I took a proper look at him and commented that his eyes looked yellow. My concern was deflected. As the day continued it became more apparent that something was wrong; he wasn't just in pain, he was in agony, and the fact that we were able to see it spoke volumes as he tends to hide being unwell. By the end of Christmas lunch my dad looked grey and my husband and I shared worried looks across the table. Later we heard him vomiting and when questioned he admitted that the pain got so bad it made him sick but then the pain would go away. None of what he was describing sounded like the musculoskeletal issue that he kept trying to assure us it was. It was obvious to everybody that he needed to see a doctor, but according to my mum he was actively refusing and when challenged he just kept telling her that the doctors weren't seeing people anyway because of COVID. The realisation that we were going to have to try and force him to seek medical help was not pleasant. I was worried, and annoyed. If I hadn't been so religious about avoiding my parents I'd have seen his decline earlier. Later that night I found my dad in the kitchen washing dishes. I put a mask on, snuck up behind him and wrapped my arms around his waist and just leant in against his back for a cuddle; he felt far too thin, and it left me with a bad feeling. In between Christmas and New Year my mum persuaded him to talk to the doctor by phone and he prescribed medication to help with what he presumed to be arthritis in his spine. His symptoms and lifelong-habit of beer drinking pointed to something more serious, but we agreed we'd give the tablets two weeks to see if they made a difference.

The year from hell ended with snow; that clean, crisp white snow that sparkles and encourages the child within to come out and play, and we spent our evenings outside engaged in snowball fights. At Hogmanay we stayed home, drank champagne, ate nice food and sampled the batch of sloe gin that my sister-in-law made during lockdown. We watched old comedy favourites; laughing until tears ran down our face and we couldn't breathe. I spent time calming down angry friends who'd had their second vaccination appointments cancelled after the JCVI changed the guidance and announced that vaccines would be provided 12 weeks apart to ensure that more people could receive their first doses due to the rate at which the Kent variant was increasing. I understood their anger as they'd consented to the vaccine based on a three-week interval and were now being forced into participating in a mass natural experiment that they hadn't consented to, whilst simultaneously finding myself defending the public health principle that was being put into place. As they knew my professional background they asked if I would mind reviewing the papers on vaccine efficacy and putting information about protection levels after one dose into lay terms for them. I promised I would do it when sober; hoping that the key messages were reassuring. At midnight the surprise fireworks from Stirling and London made us smile, and left us feeling grateful for this little gift of normality. As Auld Lang Syne played I found myself crying as although the vaccines provided hope it just seemed so hard to imagine that we would ever return to that life where it was socially acceptable to have your hand grabbed by a stranger and be pulled into a hug to celebrate the promise of new beginnings. After the bells we found ourselves participating in an unscheduled, drunken Zoom call with my brother- and sister-in-law. The call was filled with discussions about all of the things in the last year that we could be grateful for. Not only had we survived 2020 with our physical health intact, but we had roofs over our head, money in our bank accounts, were surrounded by love and we'd learnt to savour living in the moment and the simple pleasures of being outside. Yes, our mental health had taken a bruising, but we were still standing. Nobody dared to say that 2021 would be better; all preferring to reserve judgment until it proved itself not to be as much of a shit show as 2020 had been. But there was hope that things would get better.

The first four days of 2021 were spent sledging and ski scooting. It felt strange that after a year of craving connection I felt at peace standing in the middle of an empty golf course tossing snowballs at my son while he zoomed past. The quiet solitude was bliss and neither of us wanted the snow to go away. It would continue to snow regularly throughout January and my phone quickly filled up with images of building snowmen, snowball fights, sledging and snow scooting with my son and his cousins. One day as we left the tranquil white space behind to go home, the reality of COVID came crashing back as my son asked *'has Nicola told us how many people have died today yet?'*. My heart broke. This was not the kind of question that a four-year-old should be asking.

My son returned to nursery in early January due to my key worker status. When I dropped him off he was the only child there but when I picked him up it turned out that there'd been three children at nursery and he'd had a really great time. Later that afternoon the lockdown in Scotland was extended until February. My mum phoned to say that she'd been thinking about the new variant and looking after my son. We agreed that I'd relinquish his key worker space and we'd live with them as we had before Christmas so they could care for him without worrying about him mixing with others. I also decided that I wouldn't stay completely isolated so that I could be fresh eyes for how dad was faring health wise.

Over the next few weeks my dad declined further. He just sat silently in his chair. He was in constant agony and continued to vomit multiple times a day. He was jaundiced and deathly grey. He looked like he'd lost more weight. He was irritable and excessively sleepy. Persuading him to phone the doctor resulted in a higher dosage of pain medication rather than the investigations that were urgently needed as he continued to not disclose key information to the doctor about his health or admit how ill he actually was. The absence of in-person medical consultations was an absolute nightmare because any doctor who would've seen him would've had urgent bloods taken and possibly admitted him for observation. Instead the GP had his hands tied behind his back by a patient he couldn't see failing to disclose that there was something seriously wrong. It made me wonder just how many families had been in this position over the last year?

While trying to work and provide support to mum and dad the police turned up to investigate a report that my parents were in breach of the coronavirus regulations by having a visitor in their home. The explanation of my job and the need for childcare led to them being satisfied that we were acting in accordance with the law. I was equal parts angry at, and proud of, the person who'd phoned to complain as at least it showed that they cared about the rules. On top of all this my son decided to join in the drama later that week by muttering the words *'I don't feel well mummy'*. The thermometer confirmed that his temperature was above 38 degrees so we went through the motions of phoning my parents and asking them to isolate, before booking a test and getting in the car to go on the World's Worst Day Out. Fortunately, the results were negative.

When dad's blood tests came through a week later he was called to the surgery for an immediate re-testing. When I saw the biochemistry results my skin ran cold as I noticed not only the number of abnormal values, but just how abnormal some of them were. Later that night out-of-hours phoned with the results of his blood tests and, eavesdropping in the hall, I heard the out-of-hours doctor say to dad that he wanted to admit him to hospital. I felt like screaming as my dad declined and said that he'd wait until the morning to discuss the issue with his own GP. When my mum asked him what the doctor had said he replied that he'd said that nothing had really changed and that he was fine! I snapped and told him that he was not fine as all of the chemicals in his body were so completely out of whack it was a miracle he was still sitting up and talking. I immediately felt guilty at the look on mum's face. Neither of the women in the house slept that night. In the morning I walked down the stairs with the morbid anticipation that I'd find that my dad had died in his sleep.

At 9am I was packing a bag of clothes and toiletries for dad as he was being admitted to hospital. I really wasn't sure if my dad was ever going to come out of the hospital so I decided the rules on distancing could take a flying leap, and before he got into the car I pulled him in for a very long hug. The next few days were rough. My son missed his grandad terribly and mum was a wreck. She was stressed because dad had told her there was somebody with COVID on the ward. She was stressed because she couldn't get a straight answer out of either my dad or the nurses about what was happening. And she wasn't sleeping. After a particularly distressing phone call with my dad I gave her a cuddle and then went downstairs to phone the hospital, and we had a very frank conversation about what was happening. The consultant asked questions as to what I knew about my dad's drinking in the last couple of months; my guess was that based on the timing of his illness he'd started drinking heavily when furloughed in November. He sighed and told me that they were seeing far too many patients this year with emergency admissions for the effects of alcohol abuse, including far too many people who'd only been occasional drinkers in the past, as people turned to alcohol to cope with the psychological effects of lockdown.

As dad continued to receive treatment my brother became the first person in the family to be vaccinated against coronavirus. As a local authority employee working at home he'd been approached about volunteering to work within one of the mass vaccination centres and, as it would involve interacting with NHS patients, he'd be vaccinated prior to doing any shifts. It was a welcome bit of good news. Over the next week my son and I lived with my mum near enough full-time. In fact, my son was actively refusing to leave her house as he was worried about her being alone while dad was in hospital. At the weekend my husband came and helped me completely gut my parent's house and, based on discussions with the nurses about dad's mobility, we arranged for emergency modifications to be made; the first one being getting a new bannister installed to replace the one that my parents had removed years ago. I drove my mum to her own outpatients' appointments, and on the drive back I told her that we were officially forming a bubble on the grounds of both childcare and caring responsibilities. There would be no more distancing. Enough was enough.

As February began I retrieved dad from hospital. It felt weird. The place was a ghost town. Arriving back home it was apparent that the modifications to the house were much needed as dad struggled to safely negotiate stairs and had next to no balance. In between working, cooking and cleaning at my parents' I went to the park with my son and nephew, and we played in the snow. Dad's slowly getting stronger and regaining weight. He takes his medication and goes for weekly blood tests. He mainly avoids drinking, but there have been a few slips. It's frustrating because he says that he doesn't think he can give up alcohol alone but won't accept help from addictions or talk to any of us about it. My mum has now given up alcohol and I limit myself to sharing one bottle of wine with my husband at the weekend. My son's behaviour declined in response to all the stress and after a few days of trying to get him to open up he lists everything that he's worried about in the last month. At the top of the list is the fear that his beloved grandad could have died and the memories that that triggered were of those long two months of lockdown where he couldn't see his grandad. To help him we introduce a nightly routine of talking about emotions and the importance of not letting the worry monsters build up inside.

The rest of February passes by in a blur as I continue to juggle responsibilities. A close friend has a baby girl and I find myself looking forward to the days when we can travel safely to see them both. Around about the same time a former colleague is in isolation with her elderly father and his partner as they've tested positive for COVID. A week later she posts that her dad has passed away as a result of the virus. Several days later the news comes that her dad's partner has succumbed to the virus too. The news is awful and emphasises that although there is hope the virus is still out there circulating.

Two days before the end of February I spot a blue envelope hanging from the letterbox. I stop. I know what that colour signifies, and a smile breaks out onto my face as I retrieve this precious envelope. I open it and it's the first appointment for my COVID vaccine! The joy it brings is overwhelming and I sit down on my bed and cry. I genuinely hadn't been sure whether or not I would qualify for vaccination within the underlying health conditions category because just a few short weeks ago the JCVI removed the majority of asthmatics from that list on the basis that there was no evidence of increased mortality among this group when compared to the wider population. But none of that mattered now; I had my blue envelope, and it really didn't matter if the reason I had received it was because of my asthma or my weight or the combination of the two. I quickly interrupted my husband at his work to show him the envelope, before showing this treasure to my son. When I explained what the envelope was his reaction was amazing; his mouth dropped open, he clutched the envelope to his chest and he squealed with delight. In my mind I say a small expression of gratitude to every scientist, politician and civil servant who's played a role in delivering a successful vaccination programme. But I let my son give Nicola the credit for this one as, after a year of her being the 'mean lady' in the eyes of a four-year-old, he needs to see her as the amazing leader that she's been for the last year. I send a picture of my envelope to my mum, and wait for the reply message. She hasn't received her appointment yet.

Vaccine Day rolls around. It's hard to describe the intense feelings of relief this vaccination brings. As I walk into the hall where I held my wedding reception to get my first dose of the AstraZeneca vaccine I can't help but think about how this place has been the site of two 'new beginnings' for me. Yes, the future is uncertain. There is still the very strong chance that mutations of the virus will escape the protection that this vaccine brings, especially if countries continue to fight over vaccines and the poorest nations don't get vaccinated quickly. But there's hope.

With that hope comes a sense of lightness that's been missing in the darkness of the past year. And it only seems fitting that that sense of lightness is being heralded in by the lighter nights that will once again allow us to meet outdoors with friends and family, and enjoy the connection that we've so desperately missed.

WHEN HOME BECAME A PRISON & COVIDOO'S BECAME REALITY

When I was asked to write this, I wasn't sure. I'm not much of a writer, I didn't think what I had to say would be interesting or helpful to anyone and my experience of lockdown has not been particularly good for my mental health. I wasn't sure if I wanted to go back through it all, especially because it's that dreary post-Christmas time where most of us feel a bit blue anyway (especially here in Scotland when the January and February weather is dull and rubbish, not to mention that Christmas and New Year was a bit of a write-off in 2020). Do I want to pick at that unhealed wound? 2021 was supposed to start different too but we were in another strict lockdown; I was back stuck at home and not able to work. I'm alone, I'm skint, I'm in physical pain as well as mental and I'm miserable.

Then I thought, my story is as interesting as anyone else's. If mine can help someone else who's feeling the way I've felt/am feeling, then is it not good to share and let others know that other people are struggling with it all too? Writing this hasn't been easy, but it's helped a bit to get my thoughts and feelings out of my head and on to paper.

I am a self-employed hairdresser; I absolutely love what I do – it's my passion, I love helping people to feel better about themselves and I love the social aspect of it. A lot of my clients are like friends to me and it's great catching up with them whilst

I do their hair – we talk about everything and anything, have a good laugh, a good bitch and we set the world to rights. It's a very sociable job, very creative and it's more a vocation than a job. But it has caused me a lot of stress and worry because of the lockdown that I don't think other people have understood properly – unless it's affected them too.

When lockdown was first announced in Scotland in March 2020 I don't think I thought too much about it – I definitely didn't think it was going to impact me as much as it has. I didn't think it would last as long and would see me unable to work and earn money for a massive part of the year (I think I've worked four months in the past year). When I write that it sounds crazy and I'd never have believed it would happen if you told me that at the start of last year.

In the beginning, nothing was set up for the self-employed – all the focus seemed to go on furlough and supporting business. Like many other self-employed hairdressers, I rent a chair from a salon and, at the start, I was still expected to pay chair rent – even though I wasn't legally allowed to work. Me and the others who rented chairs argued that we shouldn't have to pay but the owner of the salon was operating a business and needed the income. I understand why, but the government had made it very clear that financial support for small business was coming. At least salon owners – who I completely get had also been forced to close, their income had also disappeared and they had overheads to pay – had the prospect of financial support (I appreciate we didn't know the extent of the small business support that would be made available at the start) and were able to claim rates relief, other small business grants and also furlough for employed staff. There was nothing like that for the self-employed who didn't have business premises, not at that time – and the small business support came way before support for the self-employed with no premises. On top of the isolation of lockdown

I got more and more stressed and got anxious even just going for a walk when I should've been looking forward to getting outside, getting fresh air and seeing other people instead of my four walls.

After lockdown happened, it took three weeks for me to get through to Universal Credit and another five weeks after that until I received any payments – so it was eight weeks before I received a Universal Credit payment because of the thousands and thousands of people having to sign on. Thankfully, I had some income from previous months in the bank to tide me over, but things were really tough – I don't think I can explain how difficult it was financially. Hairdressers don't get paid big bucks, we make a modest income but it's nothing to shout home about (unless you're a big famous hairdresser or have a chain of salons!) so what I did have was barely enough to pay my bills. I was able to claim an advance from the Department of Work and Pensions until my Universal Credit came in, but this had to be repaid. Also, Universal Credit is only backdated for the month so I missed out on a whole month's worth of payments – a payment I wouldn't have had to pay back. I really don't think that was fair as it wasn't through anything I did. There was absolutely no thought given really to the fact we were in a government-enforced lockdown and they just stuck to the usual way of doing things – the Universal Credit system didn't work for this and it shows just how bad it is when things aren't going according to plan. Nobody knows what's around the corner but the benefits system should be able to cope and if it can't there's something not right. I really don't know how I'd have survived financially if I didn't have some money in my bank. The relief when I started to get Universal Credit in May 2020 – I can't explain the weight that lifted, even thought it was a pissy wee amount compared to what I'd normally earn.

I think it was June 2020 when the self-employed business grants came in – three months after lockdown happened. I don't know what they expected people to do in those three months. It wasn't a monthly income, it was a one-off payment to cover us for all three months and it wasn't that big either. The issue then was that Universal Credit isn't payable if you've had any income in the month prior as it's paid in arrears (what good is arrears when most bills have to be paid in advance?). For that month I didn't get Universal Credit because my business grant was considered income (which would've been fair enough if the grant wasn't so pitiful). On top of that, self-employed business grants were taxable so income tax and National Insurance contributions also had to come off.

The lack of income made my day to day life very hard and it was difficult to not continuously worry. Money stress had a massive effect on my mental health; I was stressed and anxious about money all the time and constantly worried how I was going to pay my rent, bills and buy food; it's just as well we were under strict stay at home orders as I couldn't have afforded to go anywhere anyway. Thinking about it now, I'm angry it took the government so long to provide support to people like me and let us sit home and worry and stress about money when we've paid our taxes like anybody else. It feels as if we were an afterthought.

I love my job and I love my clients but I'd been feeling a bit stuck for a while. I'd worked in the same place for a long time and was feeling that I needed a bit of a change even before COVID-19 came along. I'd wanted to move elsewhere, but I'd kind of got comfortable and the thought of all the stress and upheaval of moving wasn't enticing, plus finding another salon that would be a good fit isn't easy. The stress I was going through made me realise there's much more to life and has made me want to achieve my goals and this drove me to looking for a new opportunity to finally make the move I'd been thinking of for a while.

Going into the second – or third, I lose track! – lockdown in December 2020 felt much more positive because I'd made this change and this will have a better and more positive end when I can go back to work (hopefully) at the end of April 2021 in a new salon with new people. I'm excited to be starting this new part of my career journey. Although the first lockdown was really tough – money-wise and mental health wise – I am a bit grateful as it's kind of gave me the kick up the bum that I needed to look for new opportunities so that's a good thing that's come out of all this mess. I was definitely getting bored before and happily sat in my comfort zone and I'll never settle for that in future, I don't think – I have lockdown to thank for that.

Emotionally I've had good days and bad days – suffering from poor mental health isn't easy. Being stuck in a small flat completely alone (apart from my dog) proved to be very challenging, I can't remember another time where I've felt so lonely. Combine the isolation with the money worries and I really was an emotional wreck. It got so bad at one point that I had to go and stay with someone else for two weeks in June 2020 as I was really struggling mentally. I think the sociable aspect of my job has made things more difficult for me as I think the loneliness is worse because I chat away all day to lots of different people and having that taken away is hard – and I live alone. I think, when you're not allowed to do something it really makes you want to do it all the more, and it makes you miss people who you're desperate to see like crazy.

My mental health took another nose-dive around July 2020, I think, when I found out that my boyfriend of nine months who I hadn't seen since lockdown started had been seeing someone else (don't ask me how given we were all supposed to be in lockdown and socially distancing!). It was a rollercoaster. I was already low because of being alone and stressed and I initially felt really hurt, betrayed and very, very angry. Just before lockdown happened he'd been declaring his love for me so it was a real shock that he did what he did. But, after I found out all the circumstances and everything that happened, all I felt was a huge sense of relief. I feel that I've dodged a bullet and I suppose I have the other girl to thank for that. But going through what I did at the start of lockdown – which he knew about as I'd poured my heart out to him on the phone – and then adding his betrayal was pretty awful. A break-up is bad enough normally, but on top of the lockdown it was just completely shit (and you don't get any closure as you're not seeing them because of lockdown). I'm glad to be shot of him now, but that was a really low point for my mental health. My moods were up and down, I was either angry or sad. I didn't work out; I didn't even have the motivation to go out and, if it hadn't been for the dog, I wouldn't have left the flat at all.

I remember when I went back to work after the first lockdown and was working 12 hour shifts because I didn't want to go back home to what had started to feel like a prison. Returning to work after the first lockdown was a huge boost for me mentally as I was back doing what I love and making others feel better in themselves. Whilst I'm not enjoying this lockdown I think having my new workplace to look forward to has really helped me stay more positive. I can't wait to see all my lovely supportive clients again and, when this is all over, I look forward to looking back over all the covidoo hair I've had to fix (seriously, you should see some of the messes that people have come in with after trying to do their hair at home!).

Having the dog was a blessing as she's really helped me through the isolation and loneliness as she was my main source of company for months on end and forced me to get outside for a walk, even when I really didn't want to. Everything does seem better when you've been out for a walk. She boosted my mental health, for sure, and I don't know what would've happened if I didn't have her – she's saved me! I do think though, that this extreme loneliness means I now appreciate everything more as it's shown me all the little things in life that I've been taking for granted.

Lockdown number one was awful and I've figured out what to do to keep myself upbeat and positive. Changing up my work is a big part of that, for sure, but there were other things I did too that have helped.

I've always liked to think of myself as pretty house-proud but this has taken on a whole new meaning during lockdown. Well, after COVID-19, my flat is immaculate. I decorated, de-cluttered, tidied and became a DIY queen; I don't ever want to see another piece of flat-pack furniture! I was always finding something to chuck out or reorganise. I kept myself busy and focussed on getting all the jobs done that I used to say *'I'll do it tomorrow'* about. Now my flat is lovely; all decorated, very clean and decluttered. That's definitely one of the benefits of lockdown – even if I did have to do it to keep my sanity.

Because I didn't work out during the first lockdown and really suffered, I've learnt my lesson. I'm doing regular work outs now and I've got a friend who FaceTime's me to 'encourage' me (i.e. bullies me into doing it with her!) so that I don't cop out. I've also gutted my wardrobe and I've so many outfits that I want to wear when this is all over so this is giving me the motivation to work out. Getting outside is also something I've done more of and I don't feel like it's a chore anymore but something I want to do.

I also joined Tinder in summer 2020 after my ex and I broke up. I met someone (first time I've ever done online dating!) and we get on really well so we've been chatting which is nice. We've also met up a few times but I'm being really relaxed about it and we're sticking to the restrictions. Who knows if it'll go anywhere, I'm taking it a day at a time and have just been enjoying chatting to someone different.

The last thing I want to say is about mental health. Mine has been really bad and I've also had problems with back pain that's been really hard to live with which has made things worse. It got so bad in early 2021 I went to my GP and spoke to her a few times about how I was feeling and she gave me some things to do to try and help me cope, but none of it worked. It was getting worse and worse and nothing I was doing was making it better. I've been on antidepressants before but they didn't help and mucked up my sleep so when the doctor suggested I try them I wasn't sure. Because of the NHS restrictions and COVID-19, the waiting list for any kind of mental health service is long so there's no chance I can speak to someone without having to pay for it myself (and I'm still skint as I can't work!). Eventually I agreed to try the antidepressants. At the moment, there's not much else I can do. I don't know yet if they're making a difference but I'm making an effort every day to try and be more positive, appreciate what I do have and I'm trying to look forward to life after COVID-19.

THE LOWEST OF LOWS & THE HIGHEST OF HIGHS: A LOCKDOWN OF TWO EXTREMES

In January 2020, I recall watching news from China of a new virus with first Wuhan, then the whole country going into lockdown. At that time, I didn't think for a moment that it would have any major impact on my day to day living and went about my life as normal which, unfortunately, wasn't a particularly happy time regardless of what was being shown on the news.

During the second week of January I accompanied my mum to her oncology appointment where we were told that after nearly three years of battling her cancer, there was no more that could be done and she was given a prognosis of three to four months left to live. At the same time my maternal grandmother, who was already physically disabled and completely reliant on her family for personal care, deteriorated further due to vascular dementia. Our family had to make the very difficult decision to seek help and sought residential care for her in a nursing home.

As the weeks progressed, family members were taking it in turns to travel to look after my mum who was staying on her own at home whilst also visiting my grandmother in her care home in a different town. My last visit to my grandmother was during the second week of March when my husband and I unfortunately found her in a very distressed state and her physical condition was, to be blunt, neglectful. I made a formal complaint to the care home and spoke to my other family members where we all agreed we would keep a very close eye on her care in the home. Little did we know that the following week visits to care homes would be stopped and I would unfortunately never see my grandmother alive again.

The next week after worryingly high numbers of deaths being reported due to the spread of the virus, the whole of the UK went into lockdown. What followed was the same for many people: home schooling my six-year-old son; worrying about coming into contact with anyone outside of my household; and the never-ending uncertainty as to the real extent of the danger of this novel coronavirus to our health and our lives. I have psoriatic arthritis and the medication I take to help alleviate the pain compromises my immune system so I was classed as vulnerable and told that I had to shield until I was instructed otherwise. My husband and I followed all the guidance but there was no way I could stay away from visiting my terminally ill mum. I scheduled my visits really carefully so that I didn't turn up at my mums at the same time as any other members of my family. We limited ourselves to only visiting in her back garden and forced ourselves not to give her the hugs we so desperately wanted to in fear of unwittingly passing the virus to her or vice versa. There were many times that my mum needed extra care for pain management but she refused to go into the hospital as she was advised that she would not be allowed any visitors and she couldn't bear not to see her family in her last few weeks and months of her life.

During this time, I was also working from home myself, home schooling my son and we still had the worry of my grandmother's treatment in the care home. Follow up appointments to the care home by professionals did nothing to alleviate our concerns over my grandmother's care and, because of the prohibition of visitors to care homes, we had the constant worry of how she was and feeling incredible guilt at not seeing her to check that she was being properly cared for ourselves. My son and I wrote letters to her telling her how much we loved and missed her and hoping she understood the reason why we were not able to visit. However, in her confused state, I fear she felt completely abandoned in her last few months with us and feel certain that not seeing familiar faces sped up her demise. My grandmother, who was the centre of our family, a huge personality who spent her entire life caring for her family, passed away in August 2020 in the care home completely alone with no family around to comfort her or hold her hand in her final moments. There is a deep guilt and regret that I will carry with me for the rest of my life.

My mum lived a few months longer than initially predicted, however, by July she really started to fail. I recall speaking to her GP on the phone who asked me to convince my mum to let them admit her to hospital. By this point, as COVID numbers had started to fall, patients were now allowed to have one named visitor. No matter how much we begged, my mum again refused to be admitted, citing the fact that she was unable to choose between which of her children or her brother would be the one who would be allowed to see her. By the end the choice was taken out of her hands and my mum's last few weeks were spent in a hospice. The day after mum was admitted into the hospice, my grandmother passed away. I recall sitting outside the hospice with my sister pleading with the nursing staff to allow us in to see her so that we could tell her in person that her mum had died. We were not allowed in to visit her until her coronavirus test result had come back with a negative result and, although we understand the reason why we were not allowed in, it was so incredibly frustrating and worrying. My mum had her mobile phone with her and we were terrified that she would find out over the phone by someone else calling with their condolences.

By August mum was too ill to attend her mother's funeral so had to watch it via a live link from her own hospice bed. Being unable to be there with her family or say goodbye in person was just heart breaking and I can't even begin to comprehend just how that must have felt for her.

My mum lived for just over a month after my grandmother's death before she also passed away. Thankfully, in the last few weeks of mum's life, her immediate family were allowed to visit but numbers were limited because of the virus. This meant that some of her grandchildren were not able to visit her in her last few weeks so she never got the chance to see any of them again, nor did they get the chance to say goodbye. The hospice was, understandably, very strict with visiting until the day she died. I will be forever grateful that my uncle, myself and my siblings were able to visit mum and be there with her during her final hours. However again, due to COVID, we were restricted to two visitors at a time and we were not allowed the use of the family room inside of the hospice, instead waiting in the car park, socially distancing until it was our turn to see her. I am so thankful that I was with mum during her final moments and was able to give her a hug and kiss just before she slipped away – something my mum was unable to do for her own mum. It's such a small thing really that we take for granted but when you can't do it you realise how important that goodbye actually is.

As with my grandmother's funeral there was a maximum of 20 people allowed at mum's funeral, all wearing masks, social distancing being adhered to and no wake to celebrate her life and mourn our loss. I was unable to hug my brothers or my sisters, all of us having to sit in our own family groups and having to leave the premises immediately after the service ended. Friends and family watched mum's and my grandmother's funerals' online but it wasn't the celebration of their lives that either of them deserved. I am writing this in

February 2021 and we still have their ashes to bury as per their wishes but, due to further restrictions, we have so far been unable to do so. With the restrictions on how many adults can gather at one time and from different households, we have had to delay taking them to their final resting place as the whole family want to be together to say a final goodbye in a way that befits the amazing women they were.

I don't think it will come as a surprise to say the lockdown of 2020 impacted mine and my families' lives in a way I couldn't have imagined. Although there was also the stress of working from home, home schooling and shielding along with the general concern about the virus, all of that was eclipsed by the loss of my mum and grandmother. Their deaths were not COVID-19 related, and would've happened regardless. But, not being able to spend the time with them, hug them, see them whenever we wanted to, spend time as a family, able to come together in the family room at the hospice, having to wait outside in the car park for our turn to say goodbye and then not being able to have a proper funeral and celebration of their lives was horrendously painful and a matter of continued deep sorrow and regret. We all understand why these restrictions are in place, but it doesn't deter from the fact that they deserved more.

Although there was a tremendous amount of pain and heartache for my family in 2020, the year ended on a massive high for my husband and I by welcoming our second child into the world in the middle of December. Throughout my pregnancy there was always the added concern of catching the virus and the worry of risk to my unborn son and I definitely felt a lot more vulnerable. During the first wave I heard how fathers were not allowed to attend the birth or visit the mother and baby in the ward afterwards and I was so worried that this would be the case for us. My husband was only able to attend one scan with me as children were not allowed in to the hospital department and so he had to stay outside with our eldest son while I went in myself.

After the birth of our son, we were not allowed any visitors and our eldest son was not allowed to come in to the hospital with my husband to see his brother or to take us home. It's little moments like that that we will never get back but in the grand scheme of things we were incredibly lucky that our son was born healthy and the treatment and care we were given by all NHS staff during this time was just outstanding.

2020 was a rollercoaster year full of the lowest lows and the highest highs. We've embraced video calling, introducing technology to our older relatives and we've learnt to appreciate the calm and quiet that being in lockdown in early 2021 has brought. We've got used to having a baby around again, our eldest son has had time to adjust to being a big brother and we've had time to get used to being a family of four. After a truly awful year, that stillness is something we really needed to just 'be'. Going through what I did during lockdown has taught me the value of family and how important it is to show them you love them all the time – we shouldn't wait until special occasions or their final days. I take comfort that I had a close relationship with my mum and my grandmother and they knew how much I loved them, even if I wasn't able to be there with them in their final days.

As much as I'd have always been overjoyed at the arrival of our son, the difficulty we've faced has made it all that much more miraculous and joyous. The birth of a baby is always a happy occasion, but after such personal loss and the general stress of lockdown and coronavirus, it's been especially wonderful – for me and for my family. The year 2020 was probably the lowest of my life, but I'm able to look at 2021

– even with a new lockdown – as a year of promise that soon I'll be able to hug my family and friends again.

LIFE REALLY IS JUST SHIT SOMETIMES

I applied for a job as an ambulance technician in November 2019 and my application was accepted and I waited patiently to hear when my interview would be as it could take a few months. I really did enjoy my job at the surgery, but I was at a point in my life that I really felt it was time for a new career challenge – I'd always wanted to work for the ambulance service but looking after the kids had prevented me from pursuing it before, but now they were old enough and I had the freedom to make the change. Then, December 2019 brought news of COVID from Wuhan and then, come January 2020, there were reports of COVID outside of China and in other parts of the world and it was obvious that we were looking at a potential pandemic. When I didn't hear back from ambulance service I just figured it was because they were too busy for new intakes due to COVID. So, I just plodded along at my job in GP practice, oblivious to what was coming.

I remember that as the pandemic became reality things in the surgery changed dramatically. Some of the older GPs had been through SARS so thought this would pan out similarly, but cases of COVID were increasing and panic was kicking in across the world and they were trying their best to keep everyone safe, even though we didn't really know what was going on at the time. As the news of the pandemic was changing daily the way we worked one day was changed the next and then to something else; procedures were written and rewritten on numerous occasions and it was very frightening not knowing what to do for the best.

With the schools closing I was worried how I was going to look after the kids with my husband away working in England during the week. I managed as my son was furloughed and was able to look after his younger sisters so I could work. My work was great if I needed to change my working pattern and hours to suit childcare and throughout the whole pandemic, even on reduced hours, still paid my full wages.

As we were on reception as front-line workers we were given face masks and hand sanitiser early on but it took some time for safety features like screens to be installed. Telephone triage was set up and the GPs were navigating systems and processes they hadn't used before by trying to diagnose patients over the phone; those they couldn't diagnose over the phone had to attend the surgery and the GP saw them in full personal protective equipment (PPE) yet we greeted them at reception with a mere face mask and sanitiser – at the time it did feel that we were at quite a bit of risk. As people got used to this new way of living things became a bit easier to explain when patients phoned but at the start it was a real struggle as people were just used to the way things were done, especially some of our older patients. Once the screens were fitted and staff were adhering to rules of distancing and not entering restricted areas it actually felt safer than it did before the pandemic.

The majority of COVID positive patients were sent directly to COVID hubs set up around our local area which our GPs helped in on a rota basis. But in all the five years I worked there, I'd never experienced the phone lines as busy as people were scared and didn't know who to turn to for advice. So many people said that they were confused as there were too many government and TV announcements and they were all changing daily so people didn't know what to do for the best. The constant changes in government guidelines were really confusing and really not very helpful at times. Sometimes I just didn't want to listen to the news as it was making me feel worse and angry that things were being handled differently in different areas and then the Tier systems came in and caused all manner of confusion – nobody ever really understood what their situation was because as soon as you got used to something it was changed again so you never really had time to get to grips with what was and wasn't allowed.

What I did notice though was that there were a small minority of people that quite clearly weren't following the rules – some didn't even try to! – and obviously just didn't care. I get that following the rules isn't for everyone but when you see the scale of deaths all over the world and the pictures of makeshift mortuaries and intensive care wards full to bursting on the news it made me angry as you'd think most folk would be sensible enough to appreciate that it might not be affecting them yet but it is affecting others. It honestly felt like some people just wouldn't understand it and wouldn't stick to the rules until a time when someone they knew fell ill or lost their lives to COVID. Then they re-think their actions. But that's too little too late. Why wait until someone you know is really ill or has died? There are so many people out there who have been ill or had loved ones who've been ill or died and I get angry thinking that just because some people don't know them directly that it's somehow okay for them to suffer whilst they go about living their lives as if there was nothing going on. It's just selfish.

In August 2020 I noticed an advert for the Scottish Ambulance Service again on our internal intranet so I thought I would check the progress on my original application, only to be advised that I would need to apply again as they had changed recruitment platform but the new recruitment round was closing in two days! I set to work, submitted another application and hoped for the best. Within two weeks I had a fitness test and interview arranged. The fitness test was tough (I'm not one for lifting weights in the gym, or the gym at all!!) but I managed it and was so proud of myself for getting through. Next was the interview; I answered as much as I could and felt confident but I had to wait to find out whether I had been successful. Another week passed before I received a phone call and was offered the job. I was delighted but scared at taking on a new challenge as I'm just over 40-years-old but my fears were short-lived as my first day at the training centre was great and my whole experience of training has been completely fantastic – I've loved every minute of it. I'm now working in an ambulance station and really enjoying it and I'll do whatever I have to help with the fight against COVID; I wanted to do this job to help people and be there in their times of need so if I'm needed elsewhere to help the NHS then I'm more than happy to do it.

This whole situation has really reinforced that my decision to join the ambulance service is the right thing for me to do and I am so proud that I can help people at what's often the most difficult time in their life and through the pandemic when they may not be allowed a family member to go with them to hospital. I am glad I can be there to provide a word of comfort to them during a really shit time.

The kids have been great throughout the pandemic. I feel heart sorry for my twin girls missing out on their last year at primary and their first real year at high school as this is a rite of passage that they'll never get back. But, like everyone else who've missed out on important milestones, I'm sure they will adjust and grow with all the changes and differences that

COVID has brought with it. My son has been furloughed from a job he loves and he'd been due to start a college course which is part of his apprenticeship but again this hasn't started. He also turned 17 and cannot learn to drive with a driving instructor which is the only thing he has ever really wanted, but he appreciates why that can't happen until things are safer. All three of the kids are very understanding of the situation that faces us, grown up with their thoughts and both my husband and I are immensely proud of them.

They are all missing their friends, but more so their grandparents and cousins as we're a really close family and used to see each other every week. Both grandparents have low immunity so need to be shielded from the dangers of COVID and the kids feel, even with being off school and work, that they don't want to put their grandparents at risk. I also care for my mum so along with the new job, the kids and lockdown, it has definitely been somewhat trying at times. I coped pretty well in general though, probably because I was still working at the surgery and then in training so I was seeing quite a lot of people. As a very sociable person myself with a wide circle of friends I was heartbroken for all the people stuck at home alone and I felt really terrible for the people home alone with no one to help them or support them through the lockdown.

Like everyone else, I have enjoyed Zoom quiz nights with friends and family but missed my mums 70th birthday and my sisters 50th. We tried to remain positive and we will celebrate another time – the most important thing is that everyone stays safe. Funnily enough, even with a chaotic working life, we have enjoyed more family time as weekends are usually filled running here, there and everywhere, but during lockdown the kids don't have their activities, can't visit friends or go anywhere so it's been enjoyable to relax with the kids and watch movies or cook together.

As both my husband and I are key workers, our girls went back to school in 2021 even though Scotland went back into lockdown. Most kids probably hated it, but the girls actually asked to go to school as home learning isn't great when you live out in the sticks with rubbish Wi-Fi!

I miss all my friends and family but know that what we're doing is right to protect others and I know we can make up for lost time soon. But not everyone is so lucky and my heart goes out to those who have suffered and lost loved ones during the past year or who are still recovering from the effects of COVID. It also saddens me that those who've lost their lives have not had the send-off they wished. In November 2020, we had a bereavement when an extended family member was killed on his way home from work by a drunk driver. We are all heartbroken for the family and for his two-year-old son who is left behind with no daddy. Life really is just shit sometimes and we can't do a thing about it but just be there for whoever needs us. I think this is part of what COVID has drummed home in us all – that we have to be there for people and support them through the good and the bad. The things you miss most are the things you take for granted – going to my mums for a cuppa, going for a coffee with a mate, having a night in with the girls, being able to say goodbye at a funeral. We just expect them to happen and now they've been taken away. That's been one of the hardest things.

COVID and lockdown has taught me a lot, first and foremost how important my family is and how much spending time with them brings happiness. My family is, without doubt, the most important thing in my life and I would do anything to protect them from this horrible virus and the effects it can have, even on otherwise healthy people.

We're now in March 2021 and I just want things to get back to some kind of normal. I just want to be able to spend time with my family and friends like we used to do before. I do also think that we need to learn from what's happened with COVID so we can be better prepared should something like this ever happen again!

MY TWO LOCKDOWN LIVES: THE STORY OF AN A&E NURSE

It's funny to think that in March 2020 we went to Disneyland Paris to meet up with some family that live abroad. Because of coronavirus spreading across Europe we did debate if we should go, and I spoke to some people I trusted at work and many of our senior medical staff were still booking trips away. So off we went. We had a great few days, while there the park had their first confirmed case. The day we left the park was starting to close.

Only a few days later when back home in Scotland lockdown was announced. I was driving home from work the evening it was announced. When I left work it hadn't happened, and by the time I got home it had happened. I never thought two junctions of the M74 took that long to drive but a lot changed in that short drive. I still remember sitting in my sons toy room talking to my husband about what this would mean for our sons at nursery, his job and my job.

From then on, my COVID/lockdown life almost felt like two separate lives. The life of a mum of two wee boys and the life of a nurse working in A&E. Looking back they seem like two different people.

As a nurse our whole worlds changed. At the start we had a few cubicles with doors which was where COVID patients went. Then, as the numbers were growing down south, the predications weren't good for up here so we became a red (COVID) and blue (non-COVID) zone department. The clinic next to us was relocated and A&E took over their space, re-deployed staff came from all parts of the hospital and health care. We were ready.

Some days we were busy, but a lot of time, back at the start, it wasn't. We didn't have as many people in the red zone, (the COVID zone) as we thought we would. The blue zone could be quite settled as well (you never say quiet in a hospital, especially in A&E) it was like people were scared to come in to hospital because of COVID so patient numbers were lower than normal. It was very strange. The people that did come in with COVID tended to be very sick, and often they weren't even that old.

I still remember a man in his 40's from quite early on in the pandemic. He was just getting sicker in front of my eyes; I had to COVID swab him, the swab made him gag and he pulled out his oxygen tubing. It was just me and him in a room as his oxygen levels were just dropping. Time seemed to stop. I managed to get it all sorted and his numbers improved a bit but when I turned around the ICU staff were there: he was going to be sedated and intubated right there in my cubicle. I looked him up on the system days later, he had COVID. He lived with his wife, two kids and elderly in-laws. I couldn't not think about them. That was the first and last time I checked on someone's COVID result. I decided I didn't want to know again so I never checked again.

When COVID started I didn't have a permanent job, but in the time since COVID arrived and now I applied, was interviewed for and got a permanent job in the department where I had been a bank nurse for a long time. It was a strange thing that, in a time when people including my own husband were being furloughed, I got job security. I still remember the day I decided to apply for the job: It had been a hard day, I'd spent hours in full PPE and by the time I'd taken my patient up to ICU and come back down my face was marked and sore. I walked into the department afterwards and lots of the staff were walking outside. Had I missed something? What was happening? I went along. There were police, lots of police, in cars and vans. Then it was eight o'clock. It was the time for the clap. All the police clapped, they put the sirens on and clapped. If I'm honest I never loved the 'Clap for Carers' thing and I worked most Thursday night's so I missed it. But that night, standing there with the sirens on, watching these brave police men and women supporting us, that was the moment I knew I was where I was meant to be. I am grateful for the great team I work with; doctors, porters, nurses and everyone else. We make our department what it is and we support each other.

COVID brought with it a new way of work, a new dynamic. You just got on with it. Things changed, we didn't allow visitors in the hospital – you had to come on your own to A&E. We got through the first wave. I remember thinking *'we've done it, we're okay'*. All this talk of post-traumatic stress…well, it hadn't come. We were okay.

But then the other waves came. By this time the department was getting busy again with the usual suspects, people weren't afraid of coming to hospital anymore; and the COVID numbers were rising and coming in too. There was a shift or two that I drove home in tears, it was hard. People were really sick, loved ones couldn't be there. Some shifts nearly broke me. But I had a post-work ritual – I phoned my mum.

During COVID my mum sold her business, so was now retired. So, every night after work I phoned her on my drive home just for a quick hello. I am 33-years-old but still needed my mum and I'm not afraid to say it.

Even now, in March 2021, some days at work are hard – only the other day we let a family in to see their loved one but I had to tell them when they said goodbye and left the department that I didn't know when they'll get to see their loved one again. I shouldn't have to say that. I hate saying it.

My other COVID life is as a mum. I have two wee boys. At the start of lockdown, they were two and five-years-old. They are now three and six-years old. A lot of time in their growing up. Lockdown gave me time with them I will never have again. Because of where we live my sons weren't eligible to access a 'hub' for childcare so between my husband, mother-in-law and myself we balanced childcare. During the first lockdown one son learnt to ride a bike and the other was toilet trained. We had family movie nights, we walked the surrounding streets counting how many things we could see – rainbows in windows or anything, whatever was on our list that day. We always took a mini backpack and every so often we had a snack stop for a wee chocolate or whatever I'd packed. It was an adventure for them. I made it an adventure. Yes, my eldest would ask about nursery, swim classes or the bouncy castle place but I was as honest as you can be to a five-year-old and told him these things were shut because of the virus. I couldn't be down or sad when my boys were with me, I had to keep going for them.

My dad lives abroad, I had no idea when I would see him again. My mum had just moved back to England so was closer than she had been in years but seemed so much further away even just there, and just weeks before COVID came we lost my father-in-law. Things were still so raw and difficult. But I had two boys. I would not let COVID take stuff away from them; yes, okay we can't do some things but, you know what? We can do other things.

My eldest started school in August; his school start wasn't what it should be. It wasn't what other kids had had, but he didn't know any better. I couldn't take him and see him in his class on his first day – instead I handed him to a teacher neither of us knew at the school gate. But I refuse to think that either of us missed out, I try and think of it like we just did it a different way – he doesn't know that that's not how it's normally done. My youngest moved to the big kid room in nursery – I don't know where his peg is, or who else is in his group. But yet again I refuse to let that get me down. My sons are typical boys; they're happy and healthy and to them this is just life just now. They are both at school and nursery just now and loving it. That's the main thing.

As for me, lockdown made me get back into reading. I used to love to read before I had the kids and lockdown gave me time to get that back. In 2020 I challenged myself to read 20 books – I read 24. I listen to podcasts now. I listen to them when I run. Yes, I also took up running! In May 2020, I download the 'Couch to 5k' app and started running. I have tried a few exercise fads over the years but this time I've stuck to it. Running was an escape, a mental escape from it all – I'd put on a podcast and just run. In May 2020 I ran for the first time. In March 2021 I ran 10k.

Lockdown has given me the time to run, the space to do it. I have used my time when I run to listen to podcasts. Running has not been all easy, there were times when work shifts, childcare or the good old Scottish weather got in the way. But I've discovered that I love it and I've now signed up to do the Glasgow half marathon in October 2021. I was born with a congenital lung problem. I never thought I could run like this but lockdown has given me the time to learn that yes, I can! I'm grateful for that.

I am more determined than ever in my belief that only I can control how I experience life and I will do just that. So yes, COVID has been hard. There are days I find motherhood, nurse life, all of it, hard. But I will not let those feelings overwhelm me. I will process them, think on them for a moment and move on. I am so thankful for my sons who keep me busy and my husband who is my biggest child but more so my biggest support. It's been hard but I am lucky with what I have.

LOCKDOWN IN LIMBO: A MERRY-GO-ROUND OF DESPAIR

When asked if I would reflect on my experiences and feelings of the first lockdown of 2020, I was unsure: how could I go back to the loneliest and darkest chapter of my life? I can't talk about my experience of lockdown without talking about the end of my marriage – a decision I made in early 2020 before the pandemic was even on my radar.

I was confident in my decision after a very bumpy road travelled to this point and just wanted to protect my children and keep them happy, safe and secure. The decision was made, although I hadn't told anyone yet. In February 2020 the anxiety around my decision was overwhelming and I confided in my family and a few very close friends that my marriage was over. These special people in my life had been privy to the fact that I'd been struggling but possibly not the extent of it as I normally suffer in silence. Our gorgeous family home that I loved that was full of treasured family memories was valued, the home report completed and it was spruced up for the photographs for the particulars which were taken late February. I saw a lawyer regarding the legalities of separation and a mortgage adviser to plan ahead to buying a new home for me and the kids – the ball was rolling!

Then in early March, the worst possible scenario imaginable – just as we were about to put our house up for sale and our separation agreement was being put together…lockdown!! All I could think at the time was: *Are you kidding me? This has got to be a joke?* There would be no house going up for sale, no separating, no escape from the overwhelming unhappiness, no moving forward. I was devastated. COVID-19 had reared its ugly head and was here to stay for the foreseeable future. *What was I going to do? How was I going to cope? How was I going to survive this?* There had been hope, for a while. It was like a carrot had been dangled in front of me and then taken away. The disbelief was unbearable, what little strength I had mustered up to find a future to move forward had evaporated almost instantly. This was the onset of the darkest, loneliest, and hardest period of my life.

Ask anyone who's been through a marriage breakdown and they'll tell you how it consumes all your emotions and all your time. My husband had become what felt like a stranger in many ways to me, I was grieving the loss of my marriage and the life we'd planned and I hated being dishonest with our extended family and the friends we hadn't already told, and most importantly, our children. But we'd decided not to tell the children until the house had been sold to protect them from the news for as long as possible so we kept the news to just this small circle of friends and family so the children didn't inadvertently find out through the grapevine. Looking back, although it was hard to keep it from them and from my wider group of friends, I am thankful we did as lockdown was hard enough for them without adding the looming thought that they would soon be living between two homes.

Not only had I just made the biggest decision of my life just as a global pandemic kicked in, I was also in the final months of completing a degree and working in a new role in a sector which had really ramped up due to the COVID-19 restrictions. For the first few months of lockdown the days were long and very tiring, with work during the day and studying in the evening. That sinking feeling just got worse; the frustration kept on building. As the months went on the burden that I was carrying around – knowing what lay ahead for us all and how I was going to shatter my children's world – just kept on getting heavier and heavier. I remember saying to a good friend: *'it feels like I am a child on a merry-go-round and I'm never getting off'*. I was just going around and round and down and down. Never stopping.

The children were off school, which they were delighted about and the sun was shining. My husband had been furloughed so he home schooled the children, which probably saved my sanity. I think, in hindsight, if I'd had to deal with the kids and schooling that would have tipped me over the edge. So, although I was unhappily stuck in the family home with the husband whom I was separating from, that was a positive of us still being under the one roof and I'm thankful that he took on that role as I really don't think I could have done it all myself. However, that comes hand in hand with the impact on my state of mind which, at the time, was really suffering.

Throughout those summer months of lockdown in 2020, the kids and their dad played together in the garden in the afternoons, building dens and eating ice lollies, they went on walks and baked cakes, went on bike rides and spent so much quality time together. While it was nice for him and the kids, I was slowly festering away upstairs in the bedroom working hard and trying to manage my declining mental health, only coming down at lunchtime and once work had finished. I would find myself sitting at dinner with nothing to contribute, listening to my children tell me about the fun day that they'd had with their dad. I'd then have to go back upstairs to study for my final essay submission which left me feeling like I was drifting further away from my kids. I honestly felt like I was sleepwalking through the days and nights – they were endless.

During these months, the negative feelings I had towards my husband grew as that feeling of dread, sad and being lost just would not shift – I felt that I should be investing my time in my children because I knew the bombshell that was about to be dropped on their happy wee worlds. But instead I found myself drifting further and further all the while watching my husband basically caring for them from sunrise to sunset. I was gutted and devastated, not because of the time he was spending with them, but that I knew what we were about to do to the kids. All I could think as it went around in my head was that he was getting to spend all this time with our children before we shatter their worlds whilst I was festering away, sinking further into despair and consumed with worry and anxiety about how they'd take it when we told them.

The weekends were no better. Studying prevailed and I really had no time to spend with my children and, during the time that I did have, I was irritable, sad, exhausted and frightened. I would watch them playing in the garden laughing, thinking how happy they were, how lucky I was to have two children with such beautiful souls, but then the crushing feeling of what was going to happen to them when we told them what was coming. I missed my nearest and dearest friends massively. Yes, they were absolutely always there for me at the end of the phone but I *needed* to see them – I was broken and spiralling out of control which is not in my character at all. I knew my friends would hold me up and give me strength. To just get a hug and have them tell me that everything was going to be okay was all I needed. I so missed that physical connection with my best friends, throughout the whole of lockdown, but more so at this lowest time.

I was aware that I was losing control of my thoughts and feelings. Ugh, it was unbearable! I get a knot in my chest and stomach just thinking about it. Lockdown didn't cause that but it did make it worse. Would my mental health have suffered as much had we been able to sell the house quickly as we'd planned? Would our co-parenting relationship have fared better if we'd been able to separate quicker? I don't know. All I know was that my experience of lockdown, because we were on the verge of separating, was excruciatingly painful and the dread and anxiety never ever left me. I wasn't able to move on; I was living in limbo.

My husband has a different approach to life than me, which did not help me at all during lockdown. This isn't his fault, he just deals with stuff in a different way than me, and given the circumstances of our separation he avoided talking about it, even when I tried to speak about it. He just carried on with life as if everything was normal. This frustrated me a lot and my mood mutated constantly from one form to another – just like COVID-19 really, how ironic.

I regularly caught myself watching the news (more than usual) and followed friends on social media; something that I had avoided, but during lockdown it seemed the best way to keep in touch with them. I wonder now if that was to my detriment? Strangers, friends and family seemed to be using this time to bond further as a family, saying that spending quality time together was precious and never again would we be gifted with time like this, to make the most of it, etc, etc. I was happy for them, of course, but struggled to see and hear it as I just felt I was drifting away on my own, dreading what I was about to do to my kids, going through the worst time of my life and disappearing further under a very dark cloud. The continuous reminders of what I'd lost were everywhere. During these long months of what should have been quality time with my family I was becoming a lost soul, crying in my room out of frustration and despair. My husband and I were living as a married couple, trying to keep everything as normal for the children as we could, and that took some amount of effort. I was exhausted.

In May another blow came when we lost our much beloved pet. My spirit was now totally broken – devastated is not the word. This was just too much on top of my already crushed and fragile emotional state. I cried for days. I was so used to having a wee snuggle with him when I was feeling down as stroking him and just having him near was emotionally comforting and relaxing. I remember when we put him to rest in the garden and knowing that we were going to leave him behind when we moved – this was just another emotion on top of everything else, but one I couldn't express to anyone who didn't know about our separation. It seems small, but on top of everything else, I was broken.

Mid-summer 2020 and I was in the last few weeks of completing my degree. I was fortunate at this time to have a good friend that helped me proof my essays and had supported me through the tears and dramas of working full time, studying and coping with a disintegrating marriage (which she knew about). For four years she'd helped hold me up at exactly the right moments to enable me to carry on, alongside coping with her own personal struggles and challenges. I was struggling to focus, my mind was on my children and making everything alright again, it was certainly not where it should've been – on my final essay. I was nearly there, almost finished the degree, but I couldn't see the light at the end of the tunnel. I just couldn't muster up the enthusiasm or motivation. Without her encouragement I don't think I would have completed the degree – she encouraged me to 'roll with the punches' and finish what I'd started for my own future. I will be forever thankful for her support and listening ear.

At the start of July, we told the children that their dad and I were separating. It came as a total shock to them as we'd shielded them from all of our problems and they'd been having a fun summer in lockdown. The following weeks were full of questions, normal questions, but they made me feel guilty, worried, anxious and the tears consumed me further, exacerbated by the pressures of lockdown. I was devastated to have to inflict this upon them, and particularly so during a pandemic when their worlds were already 'not normal'. I have no words. I could not make any promises to them around how things would look because we didn't know what was going to happen with COVID-19 and lockdown. But I do remember my resolve kicking in around now, determined that things would get better – for them and for me. This was a significant turning point for my state of mind. The despair did not just disappear in that moment but it eased slightly, enough for me to realise that I would get through this and that we were on the path to getting there now we'd told the kids.

Throughout these fragile, distraught and tough months, one thing that did not change was my mind – my marriage was over and I never wavered. I recall my family and the friends that I'd confided in who'd supported me through these months asking me if the time together isolated as a family had made me rethink the separation. But I knew that lockdown hadn't changed the situation. I had decided and no matter how difficult it got, or how lost I was, I would wait this out.

Thankfully, in mid-July we were finally able to put the house on the market as restrictions had eased slightly and the registries were open for business again. The house sold within a week which was probably a bonus of lockdown. Then we started to tell extended family, friends, neighbours, my boss and work colleagues – they were unable to hide their surprise and shock as they asked how I'd managed to deal with this all at the same time as a pandemic and being in lockdown! It made me wonder whether I had survived? The anxiety started to heighten again, no creeping in this time as it was all still there lying dormant just waiting for a trigger to full blown, and now the house was sold I had to find a place to stay – and quick.

There were no decent rentals because of COVID-19 restrictions; there was nothing – nobody was moving. There was one flat for sale that I could afford but I wasn't completely sure and I knew that in the middle of a pandemic that this was not the time to make such an important decision. I wasn't in the right mindset to buy property so I asked the agent if there was any possibility that the owners would consider renting to me for six months. When the agent came back to me to say that the owners would rent it to me I was so relieved and my mood lifted almost instantaneously. The anxiety was still there, as it always is, but it was getting less and less. I was feeling stronger; the darkness was lifting and slowly I was becoming stronger and in August I moved into my new flat with the children and my husband moved to a rented place of his own.

Just to add insult to injury in April 2020, just as lockdown kicked in, I discovered a lump on the roof of my mouth. I wasn't initially concerned as it wasn't sore and wasn't causing me any discomfort but, as the month progressed, with heightened anxiety and that feeling of dread, so did the lump but by early May it was the size of a golf ball and somehow overnight I was unable to speak. I was in a lot of pain, eating and drinking was becoming impossible, so I relented and phoned the dentist. Because of COVID-19 they were only seeing people in absolute emergencies and I was first told to consult with the doctor. I was given an emergency appointment right away, which was a very surreal experience; the waiting room was deserted, it was eerie – you could hear a pin drop. I was prescribed antibiotics and told to phone the dentist and demand an emergency appointment. In the months that followed I was triaged many times and didn't receive a call from the dentist. In the end I got to speak to a dentist and was given an emergency appointment. Because of the systems in place for COVID-19, I had to see whichever dentist was working rather than my own who knows me and my dental history. The dentist drained the lump and told me the only option she would be able to perform at that time was extracting my tooth, which I wasn't happy with. My tooth was causing me no pain or discomfort and I was convinced that the problem was elsewhere. She agreed that this may be the case but that the only procedure she was allowed to undertake was an extraction. I left, still with my tooth and a lump on the roof of my mouth. After more antibiotics the lump went away, but a month later and it was starting to grow again. I then cracked a back tooth that had been temporary filled and left, due to dentists closing in March 2020. I was now raging and this was all adding to my already fragile state of mind. I demanded an emergency appointment with my own dentist and eventually I got to see her. After a thorough examination in July 2020 and discussion I was asked if it could be stress-related as this can trigger underlying gum issues. I agreed that it likely was but was told very apologetically that extraction was all that could be offered at that time as the procedures I'd need to diagnose anything else were not permitted due to COVID-19. An x-ray showed that the antibiotics had worked and there was no way I was going to allow them to remove my teeth (the one near the lump and the cracked one) just because they weren't able to perform the appropriate procedures! Thankfully, my dentist is empathetic and said that she'd be prepared to put a crown on what was left of my cracked tooth, but it would be costly due to all the dentistry restrictions and she would think about gum surgery or root canal treatment for the other tooth near the lump. It is now February 2021 and some restrictions in dentistry have been lifted however the use of aerosol generating procedures remains unchanged. The lump has recurred again and I've had another dose of antibiotics. Thankfully, I'm soon getting my cracked tooth crowned and an investigation into the lump on the roof of my mouth. I'm an NHS patient, however, after the cost of these procedures because of the limitations on dentistry, paying for PPE, x-rays and a crown I will be significantly out of pocket but I am fortunate that I am able to pay for it. Tooth removal is permanent and it can really impact your confidence; I know it would mine. It seems unfair to me that someone who doesn't have the money would have to get their teeth removed, even though it isn't clinically necessary.

It's now been six months since I moved into my flat and we're in another lockdown. Many more people have suffered and lost their lives or people they love, vaccinations are being rolled out, we are all still wearing masks, we are home schooling whilst holding down jobs and missing loved ones. Doing the weekly food shop on a weekend is the highlight of my week, but I am happier than I've been in a long time, my children are happy and life has not turned out as bad as they had originally thought. We are okay, we have survived the most awful year imaginable. I have found a little part of the lost 'me' and am building on that with self-care every day – a rediscovered love of bubble baths, early nights, yoga and good books. I can honestly say that any further lockdowns will not find me visiting those dark, lost, lonely days of 2020 – I will be spending quality time with my children and appreciating every single second of it.

ACCEPTANCE & HOPE BUT NOT THE YEAR WE EXPECTED WHILST EXPECTING

After years of humming and hawing as to whether it was the right time to have a third child, we concluded it may never be the right time. Fast forward to 20th January 2020 and we saw the two blue lines!! Baby No 3 was due 17th September 2020!

We wanted to wait until after the first scan to ensure all appeared well with baby before announcing to family; our then 8-year old and 10-year old included. Thoughts of intentions entered my head of pregnancy yoga classes, baby swimming lessons, baby massage classes, mum and baby groups, and, at the top of my list – pregnancy massage. Remembering the back ache, I definitely wasn't missing out on that this time round! Our scan day arrived – 12th March – and all looked well and we set about sharing the news. We were excited, the kids were excited and the rest of the family were excited. Then came the announcement two days later that pregnant women were in the vulnerable category for coronavirus and should avoid unnecessary trips out with the home. My husband immediately puts me under strict house arrest! But it wasn't to be long before the whole nation had to follow suit and the national lockdown was imposed: *Ach, it'll just be a few weeks and once Easter's past the kids will be back to school…*

The day lockdown was announced my husband arrived home early because, as of 3pm, he was furloughed – a word that none of us had really heard or understood the implications of before. Working for my father's landscaping company I too got to use this new employment status. Our children entered the school of mum and dad (or in our case mostly dad as mum increasingly struggled to walk): hiking and exploring the local area on daily walks; and learning alternative skills like soup making, decorating and Spanish! We joined the nation of banana bread makers (once we sourced some flour, which was worth more than gold at that point) and daily walkers. As the weather turned positively balmy (for Scotland at least) we enjoyed our days in the sun in the confines of our garden, enjoying BBQ's on many of our evenings and playing alfresco scrabble. The kids spent more time outdoors than they ever had and learned things they normally wouldn't have. We tried to teach them as much as we knew and we learned along with them as we went. It was actually, in hindsight, a really relaxed and enjoyable time, akin to our own childhood's in lots of ways.

For the first of our lockdown birthdays we enjoyed a day of carnival themed games using props we had made and painted beforehand, eating homemade candy floss and hotdogs and the birthday cake my daughter made for herself. She accepted there wouldn't be the trampolining party with her friends that she had hoped for but she dealt with it very well and made do with us and video messages from family and her best friends.

As my belly grew, I only briefly mourned the prospects of my pregnancy massage which was becoming more and more unlikely. The realisation set in that we were in this for the long haul and, despite some of the daily disagreements regarding schoolwork being done (or not, as usually was the case), we were actually coping relatively well in each other's company. The only real mood-altering issue that was being sent to test me in particular at this point was pregnancy cravings! I had come to accept that the things I had previously hoped for might not happen, and I can't fault my husband in any way, however, being the sole fetcher and carrier of the weekly shop there was more than one occasion when he forgot my requests. And as we were sticking to a strict one-day-a-week shopping visit this was not good news – when a hormonal pregnant woman needs tomatoes, she NEEDS TOMATOES!!!

Our 20-week scan arrived and instead of being the pre-planned afternoon-skive-from-school-and-work family outing, I had to go alone. Arriving at the doors donning my mask, answering the questions being asked by the nurse and having my temperature taken before being granted entry. Thankfully all was well and although I came away with a 30-second video clip of the baby to share with my husband and kids, I couldn't help the slight heaviness of my heart that the pregnancy experience I envisaged was diminished because of COVID restrictions.

Lockdown birthday's two and three arrived as my son and I share the same birthday. This was spent with a picnic and an afternoon playing at a secluded pebbled beach by the river that my husband and the kids had discovered on one of their many biking excursions, rather than the usual annual double celebration family BBQ we usually host. But, we had a fantastic day, obviously we missed spending it with our family and friends, but we were getting used to our time in our little bubble; although I did wonder afterwards if we should have invited the Amazon and Hermes delivery men along to join us seeing as we'd seen them more than our family at this point!

Things started to look up come July 2020 when we were graced with a brief interlude from lockdown to meet up with family and friends. I was finally allowed out of the confines of our home and, for a few months, I got to savour the joy of shopping for myself once again and enjoying meals out, taking advantage of the Eat Out to Help Out scheme and just generally seeing other people. Highlights included seeing our friends and their new baby girl and another was visiting my mum for her birthday as, despite her daily phone calls, living alone she had missed the children terribly. It really is the small things that stick in my mind the most about those few months of relative freedom and the enjoyment we got from them was priceless. We also heard that the Community Midwife Unit had reopened meaning my first choice for delivery was back on the table and I was so glad. Then the news that birthing partners were once again allowed to attend for the duration of their labour. Yippee! I hadn't much relished the thought of early labour alone; it didn't feel right that my husband wouldn't be there during the whole labour. So, I was relieved and happy at that. And the kids were getting back to school at last so things were finally going in the right direction and were looking up!

My September due date came and went and the word had already begun of restrictions getting tightened once again...I just desperately wanted the baby to arrive before tighter restrictions were placed on birthing partners attending during labour. Our wedding anniversary arrived and still no sign of baby. I had a routine midwife check up in the morning which I came away from feeling down and completely deflated; already five days overdue I had thought we would chat about possible induction dates only to be told this would be done at my next appointment in another weeks' time! Fed up and sore my husband and I went out for anniversary afternoon coffee and cake before the kids came out of school. That evening after all the housework was finished and the kids were doing their respective activities, I was finally getting around to writing up all the new recipes we had tried throughout lockdown for the kids to look back on, when I started to feel a bit off, and as I seemed to be feeling worse every five minutes or so I had my suspicions. I didn't mention anything and refrained from telling my husband until I was almost certain I was in labour as I remembered the panic from last time, and he didn't disappoint!! After some frantic to-ing and fro-ing as they gathered things together and, at one point a lie down due to the excitement, we set off for the hospital via the mother-in-law's (who we had 'bubbled' with) to offload the children and dogs. Our second beautiful girl arrived in the early hours of the next morning, the day after our wedding anniversary.

Despite wearing their masks the entire time, the midwives were nothing short of amazing. However, unlike with my two other children, there was no meals in the day room with the other new mothers excitedly chatting, it was alone in my room; the only visitors being strangers with friendly eyes who were assessing mine and baby's wellbeing. No family or friends were allowed in (with the exception of my husband) to welcome the new arrival, not even our children which was a moment I had pictured in my head and had very much looked forward to. Instead their first meeting took place at the front doors of the maternity unit in the hospital car park! Introductions consisted of family and friends meeting her from afar, and some who even now in January 2021, have still only seen a photograph of her. Sadly, due to the restrictions on care homes, our new addition didn't get to meet her great-granny as she passed away in December 2020, one of the many thousands succumbing to the effects of COVID-19.

For me, possibly one of the saddest things, the thing we all relish when a newborn arrives are the first cuddles; and there has been none of that. I don't know when that will be, or how old she will be when that time finally comes. Other than healthcare professionals, no one but myself, husband and her big brother and sister have held her close. Everyone she does meet are just a pair of eyes; no smile to welcome her, no lips to watch as they coo at her. Only time will tell how this impacts on her.

Support groups are all closed, relying only on phone consultations and gut instinct – I don't envy first time parents, they must feel so lonely and scared. At least my husband and I have done it before and have a rough idea what to expect, but even we have hit hurdles. Suffering my first bout of mastitis, which I self-diagnosed having suffered with my first born, I called the doctors surgery for antibiotics. I was told I couldn't speak to a doctor until I had filled in an online consultation form. After spending 15 minutes filling in this form it came back telling me that I had to call the non-emergency line as my symptoms included a fever which, of course, was a COVID symptom (alongside a symptom of almost everything else). But, before I was allowed any medical assistance – even just to get a prescription – I had to rule out COVID so I had to make the ridiculous 40-mile-round trip feeling absolutely awful and wait an extra 24 hours for my negative result before I was offered treatment! I accepted this was just the way things were for the time being but being post-partum, exhausted and in pain it wasn't pleasant. My new daughter hasn't had all the usual routine weigh-ins and growth checks my previous babies had; and most consultations have been over the phone. Her second lot of immunisations were delayed due to staff shortages. It's the small things like that that really get to you, small things you normally take for granted as being easy. Not anymore, everything is complicated. This pregnancy may not be how we planned it or what we originally hoped for, however, in hindsight it wasn't all bad.

We've had such amazing quality time with our older children and each other in a way which we could never replicate, nor will it ever happen out with lockdown again. I feel we all got to experience my pregnancy and the children built, not only empathy for me, but an early bond with their baby sister as we were forced to be together all the time. Yeah, being apart from family has been ridiculously hard at times but I hope our children will remember this period in their lives as one of togetherness and some of the best times of their childhood ever.

For me, the words that sum up our experience are acceptance and hope. Acceptance of the guidelines and hope that everyone complies; acceptance that we can't change the situation but hope we get through it until it's resolved; acceptance that our kids haven't had the education they were meant to but hope we have taught them other lessons of value; acceptance that this pregnancy isn't what I had planned and hope that our daughter isn't affected in her development; acceptance that this is our life for now and hope that we return to some sort of normality someday soon.

When that may be, no one can truly say. At the time of writing we are in our second strict lockdown. The only let up of the rules we've had were for Christmas Day where we could have a limited amount of people within our house to celebrate. For us this meant enjoying a few hours of our afternoon sat in our kitchen with my mother-in-law (our designated bubble) and my parents, enjoying our Christmas meal together and sharing nothing else but presents and pleasantries – maybe by next Christmas hugs can be allowed back on that list! It felt good to have that connection for the day, especially given it was our daughter's first Christmas. Ordinarily she would've been fussed over for the entirety of the day, instead she made do with coos and silly faces from her grandparents across the table.

The children haven't been back to school following their Christmas holidays, we actually removed them from school a week early given an ever-increasing rate of cases appearing within their school. We didn't want to jeopardise both our attendance at my gran's funeral or our day of 'freedom' (aka Christmas), or the obvious possibility of putting any member of our family at risk of infection should we unknowingly get it. So, we continue to muddle on with home schooling which is a lot more structured this time and despite the odd protest from the eldest on the odd lesson here and there, we are coping okay. It is proving a little more difficult if the weather doesn't play along, however, I think having had the first lockdown already in the bag they are more prepared for it this time and have just accepted it.

Daily exercise has become very important to us throughout. We were naturally quite active before anyway, however, we never gave it a second thought during term time but we now feel it is mandatory given the children aren't walking to and from school or having their daily playtime and weekly PE sessions at school – not to mention their ever-increasing screen time within the home. Since Hogmanay we have attempted to complete a 5k walk every day. We've missed a few due to wintery weather (and yet another bout of mastitis!) but on other days we've covered much more. It feels good to be able to participate in family outdoor activities this time around, for both myself and the baby as we both get a bit groggy with lack of fresh air.

I'm not quite sure what the future holds, we didn't really know before and now it's all the more uncertain, but everyone is in the same position. I personally hope that whatever it looks like it contains more gratitude for the little things and relationships we have, not taking those hugs with loved ones for granted and truly appreciating the moments we do spend together. I hope the value we currently hold for those workers who were undervalued pre-COVID remains high. I hope we continue to appreciate the importance of good hygiene and how lucky we are to have such a freely available health service. I hope community spirit remains high and people don't become complacent as we have all witnessed this past year how quickly things can change.

For all that is currently happening in the world, I can't help but still feel gratitude. When I feel myself complaining about home schooling, I tell myself that at least our children are getting an education. When I feel like moaning at the shops being out of pasta, I remember that at least we still have readily available food to feed our family. When I let myself think of our finances and if we are managing, I remember that we have options. When I feel disappointed with not seeing family, I remember we still have telephones and video calls. When I start to grumble at our government, I'm thankful we don't live under a dictatorship. When I was worrying about giving birth alone, I told myself to be thankful we have some of the best medical care in the world.

There have been many wars, and even now in 2021 some countries are still in the midst of them. Families have been torn apart, there are major food shortages, homes have been obliterated and hospitals are shanty huts lacking in resources. So, I think we can take all the negatives of our current situation and always find a positive; there will always be someone less fortunate than ourselves. Life is, and always will be, about perspective. Yes, this year hasn't gone how any of us would've planned it but we can come through it together to show others who encounter their own difficulties in future that it can be – and has been – done.

LOCKDOWN: A STOLEN SEASON & THE GIFT OF TIME

To understand my experience of lockdown you need to understand a little bit about me and my life before March 2020. First, I need you to humour me, and then forgive me. I know that's a lot to ask from a woman you don't know, but you'll soon see why.

I've never been a grass is greener person. In fact, it takes a lot for the grass to be close to its correct shade of green for me. I'm the sort of person who cuts short my maternity leave and dreads the school summer holidays because I'm not sure I have the stamina for it, yearning for the comfort and structure of the working day. Later, of course, once the children get a bit bigger and life is less overwhelming, the regret kicks in. First seeping. Then floods. My brain tells me: *Look at all that time you could've been with them and you weren't – you'll never get that back!* I've always struggled with this brain that I have. It's tortured me for years and it talks to me constantly. Perplexing. Incessant.

What offsets this, what gets me through life seems to be the job that I've fallen into; I'm a teacher. Man, I love my job. I love the predictable nature of it because it's settled in a bedrock of predictability – the bells tell you when to eat and when to work. Hands up, I have become a comfortably institutionalised person. Not a workaholic, and not seeking to climb the career ladder, just massively content with what I do.

Which, in some ways I think is a good way to be, but in others is the most difficult in the world.

In February 2020, my husband and I took the three kids and our dog on an adventure around the north of Scotland. We visited Dunnet Head and stood at an angle against the wind at John O' Groats. We slept in a converted cricket pavilion with a Narnia Room that we'd unearthed on AirBnB, oblivious to the fact that our wanderlust was going to be stifled just weeks later. That's another lifeline for me, you see – escape. Getting away from home. Being somewhere…else. So, there you have me: a slightly tortured, wandering soul who likes to be out of the house.

Not knowing how long any potential lockdown was going to go on for, I decided it was time to dig in and do whatever it was I had to to keep this ship (aka me) afloat. This was a catastrophe. I could not allow myself to fall into the pit of darkness that swallowed me whenever routine was whipped away. I had to look at this in a different way. This was not a holiday, it was a different way of working. I admit, I went around the food shops where I live gathering items with long expiration dates. I wasn't stockpiling *per se*, but I kind of was. What I was doing was finding something that I could do that I could control.

At some point, I had an epiphany (and this is where the forgiveness happens). I started to think that maybe the Universe was giving me time back with my kids. A preposterous statement I know, and not 'big picture' thinking, but it was my ticket to sanity. Ironically. I don't mean that all those people who became ill or died or who had loved one's who got ill or died suffered for me, not at all. But, for me, in order to process what was going on and keep my mind together, I needed…something. And, for me, that something was that everything happens for a reason – and the reason for this was the chance for me to claw back some of that time that

I had lost with my children. The time that could never be regained was now…retrievable and entirely within my grasp.

Once the cupboard was stocked, we waited. We waited for the army to arrive and march the streets like the films we devoured on YouTube. We waited for doomsday. We watched Contagion. We waited for the announcement that the country was to effectively shut down, against a backdrop of cries of *'it'll never happen – they can't shut schools!'* I found myself torn. Anxious.

Then, along comes the Scottish First Minister and UK Prime Minister with their announcements of lockdown and it happened – the schools closed. I won't lie – regardless of how prepared I was, I panicked, terrified: *How can I do this? What if I don't cope? How can I do my job? What will happen to my kids? I should be more tech savvy than I am! What do you mean I can't go anywhere? What if I can't? But I have no option! Oh Holy Hell!!*

One of the biggest blessings was a friend, a teacher colleague, texting me to say he had an inflatable hot tub that he no longer needed. He was getting a new one fitted, and would I like the old one for the kids? Oh, absolutely yes. So, we inflated and filled it and dabbled in chlorine and filters until it was right. That hot tub kept us all sane. I didn't personally go in it very much (I don't care how many filters and how much chlorine we dumped in it, my kids were creating a kind of bacteria soup in there, so I was more than happy to watch!) but it was something to do that was fun for the kids, a little bit different and, when the swimming pools were closed, gave them a warm place to splash about on during the nice summer we got in 2020. We were so lucky. I count my blessings every day for my friend's generosity. I don't think he realised quite what a difference it made to me and the kids.

I didn't make a schedule. I didn't do Joe Wicks' PE workouts. I didn't even make banana bread. I just wanted to be with my children. We set challenges (who could drop an egg from a great height without it cracking was a favourite) and completed school work. I taught my children as though they were in a classroom and the structure of the makeshift school day gave me a lifeline – something I *could* control. I started the Couch To 5k; my sister gamefully volunteering to be the leader. We'd meet her at the park and do self-conscious warm up stretching, Sarah Millican harping encouragingly in our ears. I quickly learned about sciatic nerves and lactic acid from that painful experience. We followed my sister every other evening through the rural paths around the town, purple faced, hearts thumping.

I must not unravel. I must not unravel. I must not.

We had barbeques in the sunshine – a rare warm sunny Scottish summer – and the kids rediscovered their rollerblades and bikes, long ago discarded for adventures that took them away from the streets around our house. Lockdown brought them back home to play. Rainbows sprung up in windows and we followed suit with watery paints on the glass, the feelings of joy and giddiness of semi-vandalising our home taking over; because it's the apocalypse, and what better time is there?

The kids swam in circles in the hot tub. I worked. Moon sand was made from flour and vegetable oil. Painting happened. Reading took place. The world was much smaller and much less complicated without clubs and deadlines and homework. I worked alongside the kids – they settled down every week day to do their school work and so did I. I felt like a tight band that had been knotted around my brain had loosened. I had permission to be present. Permission to be at home with my children. Not just from the doctor, or the school, or the government. But from myself. The situation I found myself in, in my little world, was that I got to fulfil my work responsibilities and be a mum – and a proper present mum.

Something that often feels in normal circumstances is impossible to do.

I'm not saying lockdown was amazing all the time, because it wasn't. My husband and I learned the word 'furlough' and felt the financial sting of redundancy. Then came the relief and elation of him finding employment again. Boredom. Frustration. Anxiety. Happiness. Freedom. Worry. They all came to visit.

When lockdown seemed to be over and the world returned to a semblance of what it had been before, I found that I missed it. I kind of grieved for it, for a time. I'd got to know my children again, undiluted. Lockdown was a stolen season of calm that I will remember forever as a time where we all got to be present – it was the gift of time.

I WANTED THE WORLD TO STOP

I wanted the world to stop – just to let me catch up, I felt guilty at first, but I'm grateful now.

January 2020 arrived with me in a personal despair. I could feel my relationship failing and my partner drifting away to a place I couldn't reach him. Empty words and promises punctuated attempts to repair things all the while the painful noise in my head grew louder and louder. I slipped further and further behind my own savage to-do list of a house renovation on a shoestring budget, whilst working full-time. Putting more and more pressure on myself; I was inwardly screaming.

Early January saw a well-meaning friend help me access mental health support services. Sitting there alone in a wee sitting room, I put on my brave face and answered the 14-page questionnaire with as much honesty as I could muster. Then I asked *'so will I be started on the talking therapies?'* The answer was a distressed chuckle, *'oh no dear, straight to the psycho-therapist for you'*. I went home feeling raw and empty to wait my turn in the long queue for help.

Fast forward to the eve of lockdown. I was already feeling such despair and the growing 'pandemic' external threat felt like a strange wee distraction. Something I could relate to but somehow distant and detached. I feared for my elderly and sick close relatives. Pushing all my energy towards them and intending to 'do the right thing' for them. Disaster planning. I looked inwards. What could I control? I worked overtime late in the evenings getting as many personal and professional jobs done as I could. Then came the moment on the brink of utter exhaustion I hired a large industrial sander to finish a large job in my home that I'd been working on for a while. I stockpiled DIY supplies, not toilet rolls. Materials for impossibly far off projects so my mind wouldn't have the chance to takeover and floor me with long unprocessed thoughts through lack of 'stuff to do'. I finished building the last kitchen cupboard and, as my kitchen supplies had radically dwindled as I renovated, I tried to buy a few extras to have my – normally well stocked – kitchen up and running again after many years of living in half demolished DIY chaos. I was harassed and shamed by a scared checkout lady screaming at me for trying to buy four tins of tomatoes! Again and again she caused a huge scene at the checkout, with tins of soup and food for my freezer. I hadn't even realised there was a food 'rationing' problem looming. I gave in and left with a wee bag of food, in a state of shock. People were frantic in that first week, rushing and pushing each other – worse than the Christmas Eve food shopping crowds. I silently vowed to be more prepared and start growing my own food one day and step out of this madness.

On the Monday of the March 2020 lockdown my partner (working away and flitting between folks' homes) broke his promise of coming home to me should a lockdown be announced. I knew in that moment our future was over. I turned off my phone and worked on my home late into the night, until I collapsed in a spent dusty heap. That week, when not working I was cleaning and crying incessantly. Not for the removal of freedom but for the loss of my partner. It opened a flood gate. Rather than stop and be kind to myself it unleashed a beast of productivity. I felt such emotional pain I didn't notice the growing pain in my chest and body. The deep, deep tiredness and slow sweaty fever. I sanded, primed, undersealed, and top coat lacquered working late into the night and, between coats, lifting my dogs in and out of the bedroom window to let them outside as the newly lacquered floor dried. I didn't notice that I hardly ate for a few days.

One evening not long into lockdown, after painting us out of the back door, we set off for a long moonlit walk. I walked slowly for hours, and stopped to rest often watching pine martens playing in the 3am gloom in the nearby woods. It wasn't until I slowly climbed the never-ending stairway of the railway crossing I realised I couldn't breathe. I couldn't get any breath into my burning lungs. Suddenly the numbness lifted and I realised I was in a lot of pain and quite ill. I lay down on the floor of the high up crossing grateful no one would stumble over me at that time of night. I was at least 20 minutes until I got enough air to recover and slowly plod home. I somehow lifted the dogs back in through the window and climbed in to bed and slept for a long time. I had a bad respiratory flu for the next four days, then the acute phase passed and I was very tired for the following three weeks. One of my friends has said a few times she thinks I had COVID – whether I did or not I don't know as testing wasn't as sophisticated as it later became – regardless of what it was, I felt awful and wasn't even able to speak on the phone without getting out of breath. Living alone whilst feeing this bad was good and bad – good in that I could just concentrate on getting better rather than worrying about anyone else, but bad in that I still had to look after the dogs and force myself to look after myself. It was very lonely. But I was ill, and I find loneliness is okay when I'm ill – and, I'm never really alone, not with my dogs to keep me company and look after me!

During this time, I got word of the long-awaited counselling sessions. We went on to set up a regular video call and then proceeded to undergo the scariest experience of my life. With the help of the wonderful counsellor, we worked for 13 consecutive weeks on healing deep seated multifaceted traumas from my past.

Every Wednesday at 11am, I connected to our video sessions and threw myself into dealing with unresolved grief of losing loved ones, multiple early miscarriages, different strangers dying in my arms, abusive relationships (in childhood and adulthood), navigating mental illness in family members and the character forming ideology that gave me, taking away my ability to really allow self-care. All this unresolved trauma which had gone undealt with had resulted in painful physical conditions and bad decisions and behaviours in later relationships.

Externally I was grateful for the space and stillness of the lockdown world around me. I felt guilt for having wished the world to just stop so I could try deal with all my overwhelm. All the while the storm around me of people having meltdowns about having to work from home (no change for me), their social lives being taken away and the imposition of restrictions on their freedom and here I was – grateful. I finally had no external pressure. I could give myself over to deal with the noise in my head. It helped that I worked every day as normal and then the evenings and weekends were full of looking inward. I only stepped out of this to visit my dad and take him supplies once a week as he continued to live with terminal cancer. Time felt too precious with him to stop that.

Time flew by. When people asked in the coming months *'How was your lockdown?'* I learned the standard responses to empathise with them. Outwardly I appeared to glide through getting so much done/being motivated but really, I was learning to deal with the comments of *'oh it must be easy for you, you have no children'*, thankfully the counselling taught me how to deal with that deep stab of loss when people throw out words carelessly. I learnt to see people. To look right through their words. Trying to make real and meaningful conversations each time I came across another lone human walking the village streets or out in the back of beyond; many cowering away from contact with an unknown human.

But, on balance, I realised what a strong and vibrant community I had landed in the middle of. It took two years to actually have real conversations with my neighbours to learn to express true vulnerability (go the counselling!) and not be afraid they'd think me strange or broken. My nearest neighbours and other random folks sat spaced out on the street every Tuesday morning on camping chairs to have elevenses' like hobbits, come rain or shine and we had few glorious marshmallow filled evenings round a fire pit up in the field. I saw grown men cry when someone asked how they were, and women laugh at the relief of being away from their family for an hour. Children played in bare feet on the quiet roads, dogs charged around happily unleashed. Community activities were organised to make sure nobody had the chance to be isolated or feel truly alone: scarecrow building competitions; regular newsletters; street socially distanced BBQ (provided free of charge to each household by the hard-working community council); a local Facebook group to go to for help/connection. The sheer joy of sitting on the pavement whilst a neighbour painted my face with her brush taped to the end of a broom handle, the cold paint touching me, and people watching on ecstatic with laughter over such a small thing, all because she couldn't paint children's faces at the cancelled gala day. I learnt to be vulnerable. I learnt that its ok to be in pain and tell people, as long as you take responsibility for your own healing. I got brave enough to walk out first on those Tuesday's by myself to sit in the street with a cup of tea and not be afraid of being alone until others slowly emerged.

I got up every day, I washed (almost) every day, put on real clothes and practiced gratitude. Because I knew that if I didn't nobody else would have made me. The sheer joy of having dogs took me further afield in my home area than I ever dared go before. Crossing the once busy motorway nearby, without ever checking for traffic as it lay quiet. Wandering amongst the local hills and slowly putting myself back together. I became ever more grateful for my true friends near and far. For fleeting moments with family. Cards and thoughtful gifts sent. A time to pause, reflect and not busy ourselves with unimportant bollocks anymore.

So, don't be scared of the quiet. Embrace it and be brave. Look inwards and whilst we all clean out our most cluttered possessions, clear out a wee bit of unnecessary resentment, or rage, or forgive someone, just because. We all need to be lighter to move forwards more freely. I gave away so much 'stuff' during the pandemic – I donated, sold, recycled all the rest of the things I didn't need, what a joy to have the time to organise it all, I realised I didn't need well over half of it.

I eventually got all the DIY jobs done. My impossible list got competed because I quietly set my mind to it and felt such pride as I fixed another broken thing, created something new and fell in love with the calm clean welcoming space I was creating. Not just in my wee cottage but also in my mind. It wasn't easy and I had lots of angry frustrated tears but I was determined to have some lasting goodness come out of this time.

My advice to anyone struggling would be to prioritise your health. Eat as well as you can and go outside every day. I'm lucky I had mental health support before this next pandemic-induced inevitable surge in demand on our already stretched mental health services. I will now always closely look at the eyes of a smiley person because we can all pull a smile out, but if it doesn't reach our eyes then you just need one kind person to notice to make it feel a little better. Try it: ask a stranger if they are truly okay and if they aren't asking if you can do anything to help – just that one small act could trigger a knock-on effect that could just save a life.

I heard a phrase that summed me up perfectly before the world stopped: *extreme independence is a trauma response.* Hours of counselling and EMDR therapy helped me break those painful triggering cycles. It took a while but I've learnt that it's okay to ask for help and its okay to accept it. It doesn't make you weak, it makes you stronger.

The harsh reality of the pandemic was brought home to me through my work where I manage woodland areas. I was confronted multiple times with the horrid realities of what this enforced isolation was doing: a fatal accident from young adults drinking in the dark to evade police – kids just struggling through the enforced isolation; drug overdoses and ambulance access issues; reports of huge raves from local angry farmers; and fires being set amongst the trees, threatening all we work for in these deprived areas. It was chaos and I don't think many people would look at my job and see how much the pandemic impacted what I do. It almost felt as if people in built up urban areas were going feral: running wild around local woods usually ignored until it became the only playground available; excessive fly tipping after all the local authority tips were closed; large rats boldly appeared to eat the excessive food being left for the stuffed full ducks on woodland ponds, parents having reverted to old-fashioned forgotten entertainment for children.

But, on the flip side, the positives of community spirit started to appear with small acts of kindness: fairy trails; little notes being left pinned to trees with words of encouragement for other local strangers; painted rocks littered the path edges; the young and the elderly started picking up other folks' litter as people realised the value of their green spaces once again. A stronger community spirit and connectedness has been born from the pandemic and the lockdown and, nearly a year on from lockdown, I see this going from strength to strength. This has given me hope. And hope is keeping me going.

LESS STRESS, MORE CHILL – A KIDS PERSPECTIVE OF CORONAVIRUS & LOCKDOWN

We remember watching Newsround at school at the start of last year and people were talking about coronavirus a lot on the news. Every day they talked about it more on Newsround because more and more people were getting coronavirus because it was spreading quite fast. First it was in China and then it got to Italy and they both had huge lockdowns.

Just before our big lockdown my mum took us to London to see one of her friends. We went to see a Tutankhamun exhibition and got to see his coffin and some of the things they found in his tomb when they discovered it. We also went to the Natural History Museum and saw dinosaur skeletons and a huge whale skeleton hanging from the ceiling. We saw lots of things about space and the natural world and natural disasters. We didn't get to see all of it because it was too big and mum said she would take us back to London another time to see the whole place and other places, like Big Ben, because it had scaffolding all around it and we couldn't see it properly. We went to see Buckingham Palace and took photos. We went on the Tube, a bus and a train and they were all really, really busy. I think we were lucky we didn't get the virus because there were so much people in London and we were all close together in the museums and on the buses and stuff. We also went to Lego Land and really enjoyed looking around the Lego world and going on the rides. We liked it there because it was quite quiet so there weren't many people and most of it was outside. We had to leave early after Lego Land to drive back to Scotland because the weather forecast said it would be heavy snow at night.

Then after a while people in the UK got the virus and it came to Scotland not long after we came back from London. We watched the news every day at school and it kept getting worse. Boris Johnson and Nicola Sturgeon both were saying it was getting worse and we would have to stay at home soon. Mum told us we might have a lockdown soon, just like China and Italy. We were pretty worried about lockdown happening because we wouldn't be able to go outside or see our friends and that made us feel quite sad. But we were also happy and excited because there would be no school!

When lockdown happened, we weren't that bothered. We played around the house with our kittens in our pyjamas. Mum was working at home and it was okay as we could play around the house more because she wasn't making us do school work all the time. We loved it when we went for long bike rides at weekends, sometimes just with dad and sometimes with friends too. The best thing about lockdown was we just got to chill and didn't need to get up early to go to school or wear school uniform.

We were lucky because our birthday was in June and the rules got better so we could have a friend for a sleepover which was excellent. We also got to see some of our family for an outdoor celebration with an epic sweetie cake our cousin made for us. We couldn't go out guising for Halloween so we went to grannies house to do Halloween stuff like pumpkin carving, dooking for apples, and we put doughnuts on string and had to eat them with no hands. We also had glow sticks and sparklers outside and dressed up with our cousin. It was nice to see our cousin because we hadn't seen her all year because of coronavirus. There was no Guy Fawkes night either but there was some fireworks some nights when we were playing football. It wasn't the same though as a bonfire and a big fireworks night.

Going back to school after our very long summer holiday gave us a brain boost. Our teacher was great but sadly she has now gone to another school and we have got a new teacher who isn't very good with computers. But that makes us laugh. It was also nice to get back to play football and go to our swimming club but it didn't really last long because of another lockdown.

Just before Christmas mum got a text message from the school saying that somebody in our class tested positive for coronavirus and we had to self-isolate for ten days – over Christmas!! It was bad as we couldn't go outside at all but we are lucky as we have a brother to play with and our cats to cuddle. At Christmas we had a nice time because we could play with our new presents and we didn't need to go anywhere and we stayed in our pyjamas all day. Dad came to mum's house for Christmas and we watched Christmas films. We Zoom called family and that was nice as we could see them and they gave us some really cool presents. Christmas was relaxing and it was nice staying with our cats all day. On New Year's we could go and see our granny and grandad because we didn't have to self-isolate anymore. It was really nice to see them and get a cuddle and celebrate 2021 with them.

Before lockdown we went to stay with our other grandad and his girlfriend and he gave us lots of fishing stuff and promised we would go fishing together. Grandad liked boats and the ocean and anything to do with the water. We were really excited to go fishing with him and use all our new stuff. But then coronavirus happened and lockdown happened so we couldn't go. Our grandad was not well before lockdown and then it got worse and he died. We never got to go fishing with him and that makes us feel very sad. We didn't see him for almost a year before he died – we saw him for a little while on his birthday in September when we were allowed to go places but he was quite unwell then. Now that he's gone we'll never be able to see him again and we didn't see him properly for a long time before he died and it makes us feel very, very sad. We wish we could've given him another cuddle before he died. We can't have a proper funeral because of lockdown so we're going to get together after lockdown when we put his ashes into the ocean at a place that he loved. We really wish we could have gone fishing with him though. We will think about him when we get to go and use the stuff he gave us.

We haven't been to school in 2021 yet because of another lockdown because of a new type of coronavirus that spreads quicker. We are doing more home learning this time round, like numeracy, literacy, art, French and PE and we do Teams live meetings with our teacher and our class. They are hectic and silly and noisy but our teacher mutes the people who are not supposed to be talking to make sure we can hear. The Teams meetings are a bit weird for us because we don't really know when to speak but it's good to see your friends. We like learning at home because we like being taught by mum and dad. But people are starting to get jags now so we think we'll be back at school soon. We're not really looking forward to that but we are looking forward to seeing all our friends again.

We are lucky this lockdown because mum and dad don't live together so we can still go to both our grannies and grandads houses but we weren't allowed to do this in the first lockdown. We could only Zoom call them the first time and that was fun at the start but it got boring very quickly. The first lockdown was very strict because we couldn't go to the park or see friends, even outside. We weren't even allowed to go out to kick the football about, we were only allowed for walks or to the shops so it was very boring.

We've missed our friends. We've missed family lots, especially the ones we didn't see for long times. We've missed football a lot. We've missed swimming. We'll always remember lockdown and how important the people you love are and how sad it is when someone dies and you haven't seen them for a long, long time. We hope coronavirus goes away so we can see our friends and hug our family and go on holidays again soon.

MY PARALLEL LIFE: LOCKDOWN IN AUSTRALIA

In January 2020, I recall watching the news about a virus in China and them locking down. I didn't really think much of it at the time being in Australia. I guess looking back, I was a bit naïve about the storm that was about to take over the entire world! A few days later in a phone call to my GP sister back in Scotland I remember her telling me that she was really concerned about this virus and was worried it would become a worldwide pandemic. I recall thinking *if she thinks it's bad then it probably is* so her comment gave me a bit of anxiety.

Fast forward a few weeks and I'm at a house party at a friends' house and they have friends over from England. Things with the virus had started to progress slightly by then and there were temperature checks at the airport. I was chatting to one of their English friends as I was going to be flying to see my family in Scotland in April and she was like *'oh you'll be fine'*. I live in Melbourne with my husband and two young sons. All the rest of my family and a bunch of friends all live back home in Scotland. I was so excited for everyone to meet my youngest son who was coming up for seven months and none of my family had met him yet, so it was a bit of a special trip.

It was around the end of February/beginning of March when the realisation hit me that I would need to cancel my flights to the UK. Borders were starting to close, people were getting stranded left, right and centre. It was one of the hardest things I've ever had to do. We decided to get flight vouchers in the hope that when the borders opened again we could re-book our flights. A year later and we are still waiting and I'm gutted as it doesn't seem like my family and friends back in Scotland will be meeting my youngest until well after he turns two, if not three years old.

By mid-March 2020 the whole of Australia had gone into lockdown, borders closed from one part of Australia to another. The cases were relatively low compared to the rest of the world but scary all the same and we were in a strict stay at home lockdown with no cross-border travel and no travel in or out of the country. That lasted about five weeks. Slowly things started to open up again, the virus situation seemed to be getting better but then we hit July and the news started breaking of the virus spreading out of control in Victoria.

I recall being at work, doing a casual shift as a nurse at the local hospital when I saw a glimpse of the news that 700 cases had been diagnosed in Victoria in one day due to some flaw in the hotel quarantine process! I panicked! My kids were in day care and I called my husband and said to him *"that's it, I'm taking them out of day care as it's getting too risky"*. Later that evening I was watching the news when an announcement came through that the whole of Victoria is going into lockdown again; childcare centres would be closing as well as schools.

The next thing I know my husband is working from home and I'm stuck at home with my young boisterous boys in the middle of winter, not being able to leave the house for more than one hour a day for exercise only. This was to be the start of what life was to become for the next three months. We managed to scramble to the shops just as lockdown was being announced to buy arts and crafts stuff and general bits and bobs to entertain the boys. Masks became mandatory indoors and outdoors. This meant that, even when taking my children for a walk, I had to wear a mask which felt really unnatural when my son was just a baby. I wonder what he thought of seeing his mum with a mask covering half her face? Was it not scary for him?

It was a struggle; my youngest was still in a pram and my older son was only three. Playgrounds were completely closed for the entire time. We couldn't go further than 5km from home without a permit. I became glued to the news report daily – until I realised how anxious it was making me. I came to an agreement with my husband that he would look after the boys during his lunch break every day to give me what I now refer to as my 'sanity' hour. Each day I would put on my headphones, blast my music and walk until I had completed my 5km.

I remember speaking to friends and family in the UK who were all beginning to go on holidays and trips to the zoo. They were having parties and just generally seemed to be getting on and enjoying life again. It was frustrating watching them when we had such strict restrictions but I was mostly worried because I remember thinking *this is crazy* because we were in our second lockdown and I just knew that it was going to happen to the UK again. Sometimes I feel like I'm living a parallel life to my friends and family in the UK. We go into lockdown, they open up. They go into lockdown and we open up. The whole situation is so surreal.

One of the saddest parts of my lockdown experience (apart from seeing all the horrifying daily death figures) was watching my friend's dad's funeral online at the stroke of midnight at New Year 2021, knowing how utterly broken she was feeling at the thought of not being able to attend her dad's funeral in Ireland (she lives in Melbourne too). It was so hard. It's so difficult being away from your family at the best of times and even more so now. A year ago I had the security that I could book a flight home and be there in 24 hours if I really needed to. Now I have increased uncertainty in my life as to when, or even if, I will get back home. I continually ask myself when will my family and friends get to meet my son who's now walking and talking? So, it's been really hard that side of it, on top of dealing with the actual stress of the lockdown.

The day before my sons first birthday was very hard; I felt extreme sadness that he had spent half the first year of his life in lockdown and didn't get the same opportunities as his brother with going to playgroups and other groups. His actual birthday was amazing, my husband baked a cake and I was so overwhelmed with the amount of people locally who used their daily one hour walk to drop off gifts for him. It was very humbling that they tried to make it special as they knew it was going to be hard for me – a first birthday is normally a big celebration and they knew I was upset that my family had not been able to meet him because of lockdown. I am so thankful to them for making that effort as it did make his birthday special, even with the restrictions in place.

It's a challenging time for everyone and my heart goes out to anyone who has lost one of their own during this pandemic, especially those who never got to say their goodbyes in person. Lockdown life has given me many new perspectives on what's important in life. Family, friends and health are so very important, and I've come to appreciate the extra time I've spent at home with my boys doing all sorts of arts and crafts – picking flowers and making paper aeroplanes together. That time passes quickly so I try to remind myself to cherish it just now while the world is slower.

I feel incredibly blessed to be living in a country with strong powerful leaders who made utterly impossible decisions to close borders and introduce strict movement and social distancing restrictions to save the lives of thousands upon thousands of people. As a nation Australia has done an amazing job in protecting the economy and preserving life. Many cringe at the thought of another lockdown, and it's not ideal, but I would much rather have intermittent strict but short lockdowns, than have this virus spiral out of control killing people unnecessarily, because it could be any of one of us or any one of our friends or family and it just isn't worth it. If we keep to our strict restrictions and stick with it for a while longer I hope that one day soon I will get home to Scotland and my family and friends can finally meet our not-so-new newest addition.

PART 2

LOCKDOWN LESSONS IN COPING, RESILIENCE & POSITIVITY

LOCKDOWN LESSONS:
WHY DO WE FEEL SO SHIT?

I never intended on writing this section; instead letting the words of each person speak for themselves. However, despite the stories within these pages coming from very different people of varying circumstances, the similarity of the lessons really struck home – time and time again the same things kept popping up in the stories. I'll be honest – none of these things are new, the advice is as old as time.

Reading the stories in this book three main themes really jumped out: coping strategies; the importance of resilience; and the power of positive thinking. Within the pages of this book it's abundantly clear that it's these things – which attract little to no financial cost – that are fundamentally key as to whether people flourished or languished during lockdown.

Now, this advice might seem easy and, if you're well, it probably is. But I know what mental ill-health is like when simply holding a conversation or making a healthy meal seems nigh on impossible: I've been there and I've seen people I care about there too. If you're really struggling seek help. And if you're not struggling, don't judge those who are; they're not lazy, idle, stubborn or able to 'snap out of it' and we're not all 'in the same boat'. It's easy to say that these changes will improve your mental health but for someone who can't stop crying or is unable to get out of bed in the morning, this advice and the changes it advocates are akin to scaling Mount Everest. So, whatever your situation and mindset, treat others with kindness and be gentle on yourself. We are often are own worst critics and I'd bet you'd never ever say some of the things that you say to and/or call yourself to someone else. Compassion starts with you.

It's clear from all of the stories (and in the conversations I've had in the process of writing this book) that, irrespective of outward appearances, the vast majority have experienced some form of poor mental health as a result of the pandemic, regardless of pre-existing mental ill-health or longevity. One thing I want to make abundantly clear is that I'm no psychiatrist, psychologist or any other mental health professional. The advice in this chapter is from my own personal experience and the experiences of those in this book, and I stress how important it is to either get professional help for your mental health or implement lifestyle changes to manage it yourself. Neither of these is easy, let me tell you. I'd been prescribed anti-anxiety medication a few months before COVID-19 arrived in the world as a short-term intervention yet here I am, a year and a half later and I'm still on said medication. If I was anxious before, chucking a worldwide pandemic and social isolation into the mix was a recipe for disaster. So, it is important to acknowledge that sometimes professional help is essential, oftentimes alongside lifestyle changes. Do what you need as your journey is yours and yours alone.

Before we get to the advice I've learnt through personal experience and from reading all the wonderful and inspirational stories in this book I want to first explore why we're all feeling so utterly drained right now in early 2021. To understand this will help to put your feelings into context and, I hope, make you feel a little better. Because there is a reason we all feel shit. It's called surge capacity.

UNDERSTANDING THE STRUGGLE: SURGE CAPACITY

Firstly, I want to talk a little about the psychology of coping during stressful situations. About six months into the pandemic – and six months of working from home, alone, whilst home schooling my children and trying to keep them from killing each other – myself and my colleagues were having a moan about how we were psychologically struggling: our concentration levels were that of a gnat; our motivation had all but disappeared; the work we were producing was way below our usual standard and our ability to multi-task...well, that was long gone. After this chat, one of them sent me a link to an article telling me it would put my current ineptitude into perspective. And it did. After that, I shared the shit out of that article with anyone who complained about their focus, drive and/or their increased penchant for procrastination. And it helped them too. It wasn't rocket science and it made a lot of sense because it explained that the way we were feeling was completely normal, expected even, given the circumstances. We weren't being lazy or fickle, we were psychologically suffering the effects of trauma. This miraculous explanation? Our surge capacity had been depleted.

Let me explain. Surge capacity is a psychological term for the physical and mental systems that we humans tap into for short-term survival in times of trauma and/or acute stress. We would normally associate this with things such as natural disasters, terrorism, accidents and mass violence. To survive such trauma our bodies give us a surge of all the systems needed to help us to cope and navigate our way through stress. Think, for example, about the physiological systems which help us get through stressful situations. Humans are hard wired to survive – we've all experienced that 'fight-or-flight-or-freeze' response to a situation. This is our human instinct – we either fight to survive, we flee to survive or we freeze in fear. COVID, however, didn't allow us to do any of those normal human reactions, we had to shelter in place which goes against all of our human instincts thereby increasing adrenaline. Adrenaline we couldn't do anything with. It explains that 'high' we experienced at the start of lockdown; the hyperactivity that came with being aware that we were part of a historical event, the buzz of change and the excitement that our lives were going to be different for a while. Oh, looking back, it really was all fun and exciting. Little did we know!

Social isolation activates the anterior cingulate cortex of the brain in the same way as physical pain so your brain experiences both physical and psychological pain in the same way. Now, in times of stress (the pandemic and lockdown) the amygdala sends a distress signal to the hypothalamus which then communicates with the rest of your body through the automatic nervous system. Your sympathetic nervous system is activated first and your adrenal gland floods your body with adrenaline and cortisol to help you deal with this stress. After this initial period of stress has passed the second part of the nervous system – the parasympathetic nervous system – known as the hypothalamic pituitary adrenal (HPA) axis is activated and your adrenaline levels reduce and the levels of cortisol increase to calm the nervous system and thus your body down. However, in times of chronic stress the brain continues to perceive threat and this second phase doesn't happen. The hypothalamus releases hormones which travels to your adrenal glands (which produces adrenaline and cortisol) and, whilst adrenaline levels will drop as the initial 'fight-or-fight-or-freeze' response dissipates, the cortisol levels don't and so your body remains on high alert to manage this 'threat'. So chronic low-level stress – as in the case of the COVID-19 pandemic and lockdown – keeps the HPA axis activated which means the body can never relax or recover from stress. This chronic stress leads to the long-term activation of the body's stress-response which disrupts all of your body's physiological processes. This increases your risk of many health issues, including anxiety, depression, sleep problems and memory and concentration issues. This is why people who've experience of trauma are more affected by stress.

Normally, all of our bodies hormones and systems interact happily with each other so when we experience an imbalance in one, it screws with the whole system so to speak. Lockdown has literally fucked with us on a biochemical level, and those who are 'touched starved' will have suffered the most as the 'happy hormones' have been harder to come by because of social distancing. So, our psychological response to this past year hasn't just been laziness, it's physiological and biochemical. I hope that makes you feel better; I know it did me!

Physiologically, we experience adrenaline and cortisol boosts to help us survive. It is an injection of hormones into our internal systems that help us to cope with trauma. Our surge capacity (which our adrenaline and cortisol boost is part of) is a short-term solution to short-term stress. This pandemic, which is stressful and anxiety-inducing with no visible 'end' in sight, is collective chronic stress and trauma. The impact of this isn't visible, it's largely internalised and long lasting as our bodies struggle with how to cope. Add to this the social injustices, political conflict and uncertainty of 2020/21 and you've the perfect shit storm of a situation our bodies are simply ill-equipped to deal with. That is, our surge capacity has been depleted.

Once our surge capacity has been depleted, it needs to be renewed. But, during the uncertainty and chronic stress of

COVID-19, there's no opportunity for us to recharge and renew. The 'happy hormones' that lockdown has fucked with through lack of hugs and connection (oxytocin), routine (dopamine) and lack of sunlight (serotonin) are absolutely essential to calming our automatic nervous system and renewing our surge capacity. So, the longer the pandemic rages, the more unable we are to cope and the more we experience depression, anxiety, stress and fatigue. Now, I'm no psychologist but I'd hazard a guess that it's going to take some time post-COVID for us to completely renew our surge capacity and if you're really struggling and it doesn't seem like these feelings are going to go away then I'd urge you to speak to your GP.

How can we reduce the impact of our depleted surge capacity you ask? Well, there's very little we can actually do about the pandemic *per se*. It will last as long as it lasts. The first thing that I think the experiences within this book emphasise is that you need to go easy on yourself. The pandemic is a time of chronic stress and trauma – if you're low, not sleeping, unable to focus, lacking motivation, tired all the time and generally full of malaise it's because your body isn't coping. And that is okay. The first step to dealing with this is acceptance. There is nothing we can do to speed up the process of post-COVID recovery so we need to accept that life – and our ability to function and cope with it – is temporarily limited. In fact, studies of prisoners of war have found that those who accepted they were trapped and that this may be their situation for a long time fared better psychologically than those who held on to hope that they would be rescued soon. Acceptance can be a powerful psychological tool.

Every one of us, to some extent, will be experiencing a depletion in their surge capacity. Hurrah, we're not alone! Any chronically stressful situation (such as a pandemic) *will* end, and you *will* get a chance to renew. The second piece of advice I have then, is to remember that most chronically stressful situations are temporary. It might not seem like it when you're in the midst of it, but there will be an end. Finally, one way to limit the impact of the situation is to detach and unplug. Whilst the inception of rolling news is an incredibly valuable resource, it is also incredibly harmful. Constantly consuming the news and seeking out information only heightens anxiety and stress levels so it is important to limit or set boundaries around your news consumption, and that includes social media. Make sure you take time for self-care away from the stresses of the situation – go for a bubble bath, read a good book, do a jigsaw, find a creative outlet – anything that will take you 'away' from the reality for a while.

So, when you're really struggling, remember that your surge capacity is depleted during times of chronic stress and trauma – accept it, recognise it is temporary and detach regularly. Remember, go easy on yourself and, as one of my favourite sayings goes: *this too shall pass.*

LESSONS IN COPING

Now we know why we feel the way we do; how can we manage and/or limit the impact on our mental health? That is one of the reasons I wanted to write this book as we have all, at one stage or another, employed coping mechanisms and strategies to deal with what we went through. This is not a PhD thesis (although it's as bloody long as one!) – the lessons within this book are not new, particularly difficult or expensive. They're fairly simple things that anyone can do (and things I wish I'd done during the first lockdown instead of all the bad habits I fed!), are well known for maintaining good mental health and they are by no means an exhaustive list.

ESTABLISH A ROUTINE

I've never been one for following a strict routine. Hell, I'm not even one for following a relaxed routine, if I'm completely honest. I think the only time I've ever followed a routine was when my twins were babies and that was out of necessity rather than any great desire for structure. I love spontaneity, adventure and thrive off change so I find a routine to be a bit of a bore and inhibitive to the sense of freedom that I want my life to have. Routine though, is part of life to an extent. Whether I like it or not I have to have some semblance of routine when I'm working and the kids are at school and afterschool activities. I don't particularly like it, I'd rather work when I'm enthused and inspired, but I don't think my employer would accept that reason as a flexible working request! Nevertheless, I most definitely see the benefits of routine and structure during times of chaos and uncertainty.

I can't emphasise the importance of routine – or at least some form of structure – enough. Particularly when you've nowhere to go and nowhere to be. During lockdown 1.0 I, rather stupidly in hindsight, did what I liked – woo hoo, it was extended holiday time! A break from the business and daily grind of life, awesome! If I wanted to lie in, I did. If I wanted to stay up, I did. If I wanted to nap, I did. I skipped meals and ate when I wanted. I watched TV whenever I wanted (when I wasn't working, that is, I do have a modicum of self-discipline!). It was great to start with, but it soon became an absolute disaster. Pre-COVID my routine was dictated by school, work, meetings, after school activities, fitness classes, social activities…it's tiring just thinking about it now. Then lockdown happened and we were all at home and, unless you had a pretty good sense of self-discipline, it was very easy to let routine go out the window. I used to be a morning(ish) person, and was in bed most nights by 10pm. Post-lockdown, I'd be lucky if I were in bed by 1am and out of bed by 10am. Anyway, the reason I say this is that it was not healthy and it was not good for my mental health. As much as I hate to admit it, routine is important; and here's why.

During the pandemic and lockdown very little was within our control. We were told to work from home. The kids were told to school from home. We were told to only go out for essential shopping. We were told not to see our friends and family. We were told, we were told, we were told…and on and on it went. Governments all over the world made massive decisions that curtailed our freedoms to protect public health and that left a lot of us flailing about like fish out of water, myself included. Overnight we went from a life of structure to days and days and days of nothing but the same four walls and the same people. We're not used to that, and nor should we be; humans aren't built to live like that. It's no wonder we've all been left feeling the way we do. I don't know about you but I now have appreciation for how people who're unemployed struggle with their mental health because it's really easy to let routine go out of the window when you've no reason to be at a specific place at a specific time. The hours and days really do just roll into one. And it makes you feel pretty shit.

The problem with lack of structure is that it gives you too much time. That in and of itself is not a bad thing but the problem with having too much time on your hands is that it gives you too much time to think. And thinking gives you too much time to dwell and ruminate. Dr Rachel Goldman, clinical assistant professor at NYU School of Medicine explains:

"When people don't have a routine or structure to their day it can cause increased stress and anxiety, as well as overwhelming feelings, lack of concentration and focus...[they] are sitting around with less to focus on, then they also probably will find themselves thinking about the stressful situation more, which can also lead to additional stress and anxiety."

So, if you want to avoid the negative cycle of rumination on the source of your negative feelings, keeping yourself busy and having a routine for your day is essential. This isn't to say that you forget about the source of your unhappiness or distress – that may require professional help and it's always best to deal with that sooner rather than later – but your day to day life is something completely within your control to change to help you feel more in control and less anxious. Don't just take my word for it, the mental health benefits of implementing routine into your life is backed up by many studies and a quick internet search will find you oodles of them.

From people's stories in this book and anecdotal evidence I've realised that the people who fared better psychologically during lockdown are those who implemented routine and structure into their never-ending Groundhog Day existence. Why? Well, that feeling of control at a time where we have no control over anything else during the pandemic is something that's within our gift to change. I know a lot of my friends who coped better with lockdown did so because of routine whilst my routine went out the window and I found myself back in a dark place that I really didn't want to revisit. Go back and read the story of the teacher who, at the thought of lockdown, went into panic mode and implemented a routine to help her cope. Look at the stories in this book from people who worked outside of the home throughout the pandemic and their realisation that they're appreciative of the structure and 'normality' it's provided. So, routine brings control, predictability and certainty in times of stress and anxiety. And that's not all, because routine can also increase productivity and motivation so you'll be more organised and more focussed.

I'm not going to tell you how to structure your days, it'll look different for everyone depending upon your work, whether you have kids, how old your kids are, your caring responsibilities, what your hobbies and interests are and so on and so on. What I can do is give some advice as to what others have found useful and what research has shown to be helpful: set waking-up and bedtimes (yes, I laughed too); stick to regular meal times; make a list of tasks to do each morning – doing those crappy necessary tasks first (you know, those horrid things you've been putting off cause you simply hate doing them…yes, those); make your bed as soon as you get up; get dressed; follow your normal morning routine (whatever it looks like); get regular daily exercise; and factor in time for self-care. I'm sure there are many more, but you get the gist.

Your life will be different from mine so think about what your day should look like in the context of what you need to do and what pressures you have and figure out a routine that works for you. As much as I'd love to say it's easy and you can change overnight, that would be complete bullshit. Implementing routine is hard because it is about creating new habits (and breaking old ones!). Psychologists have found that habit-forming takes a minimum of 21 days of continually doing something for it to become even a tiny bit easier, 66 days before the behaviour becomes automatic and up to 254 days before the habit becomes fully formed. And if you've no routine at all then you're needing to form lots of new habits, so it really is a question of time and perseverance. Practice makes perfect after all.

I personally also advocate a day here and there with no routine. Mix it up. If your 'normal' life had the odd day that was different to the rest then it makes sense to do that too. As much as I can appreciate the value of routine, there's value in having a day that's different so it doesn't start to feel too monotonous. Have a day where you don't do any chores, you get up when you want to, you have a movie night way past the hour you'd normally go to bed. We'd do this in our day to day life on days we weren't working or going to school and we'd do this during holidays, so why not do it during our enforced staycation? That day of no routine could even become part of your routine itself!

Although I say all this and understand it, I admit I'm still utter shit with routine. Really, really shit at it. You'd think I'd have learned after a year of living like this. It was easier when I was going out to an actual place of work or the kids had to be up for school but in lockdown it could be any day or any time – it's like that odd time in between Christmas and Hogmanay where nobody really knows what day it is or why the hell there is so much cheese in their kitchen. My kids often get their dinner at 7pm (or 8pm if I've lost all track of time…okay 9pm) and, try as I might, I just can't get into the routine of doing yoga every morning – even though I really want to! But, I aspire to get better at this because I know it will make me feel better; if not least for when it comes time to go back to actual work and getting the kids up for school! Gosh, now that's a thought…

GET OUT IN NATURE

Ah, good ole' Mother Nature; the life-giving, nurturing and creative deity that epitomises all that is good about the great outdoors. Did you know that just being amongst nature has physiological benefits in our stress response, such as lowering our heart rate and blood pressure? The mental health sector has always pushed the significant benefits of the natural world on well-being because being outdoors is proven to release the 'happy hormones' dopamine, serotonin, oxytocin *and* endorphins. Sounds like a veritable treasure trove of mood-enhancing drugs, eh? That's because it is.

Back in 2007, mental health charity Mind launched a green agenda for enhancing mental health off the back of a study which found that green exercise was significantly more effective at promoting well-being than urban exercise; with 71% of participants reporting a decrease in depression after a green walk compared to 45% after an urban indoor walk (22% actually said their depression *increased*; this is to do with the serotonergic response whereby a busy or chaotic environment is seen as a potential threat by the body's central nervous system and so it stays on 'high alert', thus increasing the symptoms associated with our physiological stress response). Access to outdoors and the natural world is so beneficial in fact, that there is a positive link between access to green space on the well-being of prison populations and on recovery time of hospital patients, both in psychiatric care as well as post-operative and other physical health care admissions.

During the COVID-19 pandemic entire populations were confined to their immediate neighbourhood. Some of us were lucky to live rurally where we could be amongst nature within a few minutes, but others weren't so lucky and were constrained to built-up urban areas with little to no access to greenspace or were unable to leave their homes and had no access to a private garden (such as in the COVID-19 epicenter Wuhan and the children in Spain who were not permitted to leave their homes at all for 45 days in early 2020). But why did it matter so much that people were less able to access nature? Being outdoors has so many benefits that it would be an entire book of its own if I were to talk about them all. Most you'll be familiar with, but here's just some of the benefits, it: increases vitamin D; relieves low mood and anxiety; boosts your immune system; helps with pain management; provides free aromatherapy (so stop and smell the roses!); boosts your energy; it's easier to exercise outdoors; increases creativity (why do you think so many artists take their inspiration from the natural world?); increases concentration; calms you down; increases life satisfaction; provides peace; and…I could go on but I won't.

In times of high stress and anxiety, such as the COVID-19 pandemic, the benefits of being outdoors is of even more importance in helping us to regulate our well-being. In 2020, the WWF and the Mental Health Foundation launched a mental health support guide *'Thriving With Nature'* to help people maximise the benefits from nature, particularly in the context of the pandemic. The sustainable travel charity, Sustrans, also launched two campaigns to promote the use of the outdoors during COVID-19: 'Outside In' and 'Space to Move'. During

COVID-19, this advice even went beyond just the general population, with the British Psychological Association producing guidance for mental health practitioners on how to adjust their practice to utilise the outdoors as part of talking therapy whilst adhering to current social distancing restrictions. With the huge benefits that being in the outdoors brings, it's hardly surprising that the COVID-19 pandemic highlighted the importance of the natural world on our well-being.

Psychiatrist Dr Sue Stuart-Smith's book, *'The Well-Gardened Mind'* which examines the mental health benefits of gardening, explains the innate human need to get back to nature during times of high stress: *"...throughout history, people need to turn back to nature at times of crisis...we recover a sense that ultimately, it's the earth that sustains us".* In July 2020, A Dutch study by Eveline van Leeuwen and Lise Bourdea-Lepage examined the impact of spatial difference on well-being during lockdown in the Netherlands and found that the more urban the area, the more adverse the impact of lockdown on mental health:

> *"...space, and especially urbanity, matters. On average, well-being has declined across the country, but in the dense urban areas the decline is greater than in the least urban areas. And although no significant differences in well-being between urban and rural areas were experienced before the lockdown, this is the case during the lockdown."*

Of course, this is a huge generalisation and there's always going to be exceptions to the rule. There will be people who love the city and haven't missed the countryside at all just as there will be those who live rurally who can't abide the city. But, we can all probably recall the news coverage of people flocking in their droves to Durdle Door, Brighton and out to the parks in London and Glasgow in summer 2020, contrary to the public health advice and government restrictions. People were desperate to get outdoors, particularly to blue space (near the water) if they could.

That's all fine and well but how do you access nature if you live in a built-up inner-city area with few greenspaces? Or, if your lockdown is such (or if you're self-isolating) that you're not allowed to leave your home and you have no outdoor space or you have social anxiety or agoraphobia? How do you tap into the benefits of nature and the outdoors then?

Well, do what you can to bring the outdoors *in*. First thing's first, let in as much natural light as possible. Natural light (i.e. sunlight) is the richest source of vitamin D available; important for our immune system, weight regulation and reducing the risk of depression (more on that later). Many studies have found causal links between natural light and a number of desirable health outcomes such as; reduced agitation, improved sleep and reduced depression. Furthermore, lack of exposure to natural light is linked to higher levels of cortisol (the body's main stress hormone) and lower levels of melatonin (the body's sleep hormone) at night time. Unsurprisingly, this exacerbates depression and poor quality sleep as the reverse should be true as it approaches bed time and we should have low levels of cortisol and high levels of melatonin. I've lived in bright airy places and I've lived in dark light-starved places and I honestly can't stress enough the difference you will see in your mood if you are able to let natural light into your home. Not only is the heat on your skin absolutely glorious, but the sheer presence of daylight (it doesn't even have to be sunny) will lift your mood in an instant. Granted, natural light isn't going to fix everything, but I would be willing to bet that a room filled with daylight will make you feel significantly less miserable than a darkened room or one lit by artificial light. Letting the outside in might be the last thing you want to do if you're feeling shit, but please try it. It can't make you feel any worse, can it? So, open those curtains (if you don't have much natural light I suggest placing mirrors around your home to amplify the light) sit back and bask in the sun. Oh, and don't forget to open those windows and let as much fresh air in as you can. No, it's not the same as being outdoors, but it's a pretty good start.

Another tip to bring the outside in is to get some indoor plants – preferably ones that have air purifying abilities such as palms (areca and bamboo), ficus, peace lilies, English ivy, spider plants (you can basically never kill these beauties!), Boston fern and aloe vera (also good for cuts and burns!). You can grow herbs indoors which not only give off amazing scents but you can use them in cooking (such as mint, basil, parsley, rosemary and thyme). Some varieties of lavender (the scent of which is known for its calming and stress relieving properties) do well indoors with lots of light (such as munstead and, my absolute favourite, French lavender). You can also grow dwarf citrus trees indoors which will give off the most amazing uplifting scent when in flower (these again need a warm sunny spot).

If growing plants isn't up your street then even having fresh flowers in the house can have calming properties, give the impression of being outdoors and mimics the feeling of having more space. Research from the University of North Florida's Department of Public Health actually found that having flowers in our homes significantly reduces stress, anxiety and worry; increases well-being, happiness and productivity; boosts memory; helps us to sleep; and makes us more compassionate. Believe it or not, fresh flowers can also help with pain management and physiological recovery from illness. Yes, really! Come to think of it, all of this is probably why I signed up to a flower subscription service during lockdown even though I hadn't thought about why beyond the fact that I just like flowers. So, if you ever needed an excuse to buy yourself flowers, this is it – and that goes for men too (studies have actually shown that women are more attracted to men who have flowers around them!). In particular, the scent of chrysanthemums and gerberas are well known for their stress reducing properties. If, for any reason, you can't have flowers in the house then aromatherapy can work wonders – get yourself an aromatherapy diffuser, some calming essential oils (lavender, chamomile, lemon balm, peppermint, jasmine, rose, clary sage, bergamot are all good for anxiety, stress and low mood) then sit back and let them work their magic.

I love the outdoors, and I particularly love being near the water, preferably the coast but a loch or a river will do if I'm desperate; the sounds and smells of the water almost instantly enable me to release all that pent-up pressure. Then there's this feeling of being part of something bigger and the continuity of nature. Being outdoors grounds me, stabilises my anxiety and just generally makes me feel calmer. Living where I do, in the heart of Scotland, has proved a challenge as I've only been able to access the coast – my 'happy place' – on a few occasions in the past year when restrictions on travel have been eased. I've even taken to listening to the sounds of the ocean or the rain when I go to sleep. So, even if you can't access the coast or head into the glens and forests to reap the benefits of nature, you can listen to it in a darkened room and allow your mind to wander off.

There're swathes of evidence that blue spaces are indeed good for the body and the soul; the benefits are less well publicised as green space but the data is clear —the more access you have to blue space the better your mental health and well-being (particularly if you have access to the coast). I was intrigued to discover that my love of the coast and all things water is not just a happy coincidence, but is grounded in science. It is indeed true that 'a little sand between the toes, always takes away the woes' and I can't wait to get back to walk barefoot through the sand and the surf, even if it is the North Sea and it's bloody cold!

So, if you can get outside and breathe in the fresh air, listen to the sounds and pay attention to the smells. Go for a walk or even just sit outside with a coffee and, if you don't have a garden, open a window and enjoy the fresh air, take a deep breath and enjoy the sounds of the birds. If there's a reason you can't get outside or you live plonk in the middle of a city where the outdoors is not exactly calming, well, there's a reason why sounds and smells are able to take us back to times in our past and invoke vivid memories – these senses are incredibly powerful and can transport us beyond our immediate surrounds. Get the flowers in, aromatherapy going and listen to your favourite outdoor sounds as you close your eyes and let your imagination run wild outdoors.

FIND AN EXERCISE YOU ENJOY

I don't think I can stress enough the importance of physical exercise on improving mental health and well-being. Regular exercise is known to benefit stress, anxiety, depression, sleep, memory, focus, productivity and self-esteem. Studies have found that 30 minutes or more of exercise for three or more days a week can significantly alleviate symptoms of depression and anxiety. This does not mean, however, that doing less than that has no benefits. In fact, the opposite is true as research has found that doing as little of 10 to 15 minutes of exercise can also improve your mood and reduce anxiety and stress. The Mental Health Foundation have, for some time now, called for a change on how we view exercise in the UK to shift our perception that it's something we 'have to' or 'should do', but something we value due to the way it makes us feel; for those who want more detail check out their pocket guide: *'How to look after your mental health using exercise'*.

The mental health sector has been pushing the mood boosting benefits of exercise for many years, but it still seems to be viewed in most circles as something you do to improve your physical health and/or look good. Whilst both of these are indeed true, the mental health benefits are so significant that there is an argument to be made that we should be first extolling the virtues of that over the physical and aesthetic benefits. Why? Well, there's a reason why there is high comorbidity between poor mental health and physical ill-health (from cancer and coronary heart disease to auto-immune disorders such as psoriasis). If you suffer psychologically evidence has shown that you're less likely to participate in physical activity, for a variety of reasons including lack of motivation, self-confidence and self-esteem. It stands to reason then that if you tackle poor mental health first then physical health will improve as a by-product. There is such an inextricable link between physical and mental health and it's so difficult to separate the two and there may well be physical reasons why people can't participate in exercise and this in itself can be a cause of mental ill-health. You can't be holistically 'well' without being both psychologically well *and* physically well. But anyone who's ever struggled with poor mental health will know what an insurmountable challenge it is to motivate yourself to do any physical activity when you feel so utterly low and empty. So, don't exercise to look good, exercise to feel good and kill two birds with one stone.

As I was writing this book, the UK's very first qualification for those working in the fitness industry was developed and launched by Dan Hancock (a personal trainer in central Scotland who focuses not on the physical benefits but the mental health benefits of exercise): 'Mental Health & Exercise Coaching Award'. This qualification – validated by the Scottish Qualifications Authority – aims to increase understanding of the link between exercise on mental health and well-being alongside providing students with the knowledge, skills and confidence to help people experiencing mental ill-health to participate in physical activity. Given the massive evidence base lauding the mental health benefits of physical activity, and now this award is in existence, it seems somewhat obvious that it was a glaring omission. Hats off to Dan for pursuing it so passionately and driving forward some much-needed change in the fitness industry: here's hoping it will be the start of a much needed conversation and change in the fitness industry.

And the good thing is that you don't need to be super fit to reap the rewards of regular exercise. It doesn't have to be overly strenuous, you don't have to be fast, it doesn't have to be in a gym, it doesn't have to be for hours a day, you can sign up to a virtual programme, you can sign up to virtual running/walking/cycling/swimming challenges, you can do it outdoors, you can do it at home – the world's your oyster really. It doesn't matter what it is, so long as you move your body you'll feel the psychological benefits and there is something for everyone. The good news is – the more you move, the more you'll want to move as the brain releases endorphins, particularly If you do aerobic exercise (add in doing that outdoors and you've got a double 'happy hormone' dose!).

The trick is to find an exercise you enjoy. I'm no fan of 'working out' but there is exercise I do enjoy (although I admit that often the thought of it doesn't fill me with absolute joy but during and after, well that's another story). I love running, but haven't been able to run due to an injury for the last few years (that bloody pandemic has delayed all but essential operations so I'm having to wait – boo!) and swimming (again, the pandemic has ruined that as swimming pools are closed – double boo!). However, I do enjoy yoga (for the mind as well as the body) which I can do in the house (I signed up to an excellent app, although there are loads of free YouTube channels and videos devoted to yoga practice) and I walk where I can rather than take the car. I do enjoy going for a rambling walk in the glens and mountains of Scotland; well, I enjoy it afterwards so I grin and bear it because I know how good it will make me feel. And, my love of being near the water means I really enjoy getting out on the paddle board and wild swimming, both of which are great exercise and I get the added benefit of being outdoors. And don't forget – there are lots of things we do every day that are also good forms of exercise; such as vacuuming, gardening, dancing and, the old favourite, sex!

Figure out what kind of exercise feels good for you and try and do a little bit of it every day. You'll feel so much better for it and as you reap the benefits you'll find yourself wanting to exercise rather than seeing it as a chore. Now, I'd better go and find that yoga mat…

EAT WELL – NUTRITION MATTERS

I know you're probably thinking *'why are you talking about what I eat when we're supposed to be talking about coping mechanisms?'* but I talk from experience that when I'm not coping very well my diet gets worse and this spirals into a habit of feeling crap and eating crap and getting out of that quagmire becomes more and more difficult and so it goes on and on.

We are all well aware of the benefits of eating a well-balanced diet on our physical health and well-being. Not eating well has numerous health implications, such as coronary heart disease, obesity, type-2 diabetes, some types of cancer, osteoporosis, high blood pressure and cholesterol and dental issues, amongst many others. However, as discussed in the Mental Health Foundation's *'Food for thought: Mental health and nutrition briefing'* and Mind's *'Food and Mood'*, poor diet is also linked to poor mental health, in particular depression and there is a growing body of evidence that we should be eating well for our emotional well-being. In fact, the mortality gap between those with severe and enduring mental ill-health and the general public is stark, as the World Health Organisation advises the former die between 10 and 25 years earlier. Now, that isn't to say its mental health that causes this early mortality directly, but the evidence says that those with poor mental health are less likely to eat healthily and those with poor diets are also more likely to die earlier so it doesn't take a genius to establish that there is some link.

As with other health promoting activities, there are a range of inequalities which impact on our ability to eat well – socio-economic status being the most obvious. Co-morbidity is common amongst people from areas of deprivation; with higher levels of both mental ill-health and poor physical health amongst those living in poverty. Now, this relationship is complex and there is no one explanatory factor as a number of demographic variables may impact upon any association. However, irrespective of this, a *'Strategic Review of Health Inequalities in England Post-2010'* (The Marmot Review) found a two-way relationship between obesity and depression: those who were obese had a 55% increased risk of developing depression; and those who had depression had a 58% increased risk of developing obesity. Another 2014 systematic review in the American Journal of Public Health found that a poor diet was linked to poorer mental health amongst children and young people. Conversely, research off the back of the English Health Survey in 2014 found that those who eat more fruit and vegetables were found to have higher levels of well-being. Similarly, a 2017 study in Nutritional Neuroscience found that those who followed a Mediterranean diet supplemented with fish oil led to reduced depression. So, the relationship between nutrition and well-being is complicated and if the researchers who spend their whole careers trying to understand it can't then I'm not going to try here. What does matter, however, is that there *is* a link.

I'm sure you're all well aware of what the 'right' and 'wrong' foods are to eat to promote better health and well-being so I I'm not going to get into the specifics of nutrition or what we should and shouldn't eat; *'The Eatwell Guide'* from the NHS is a good place to start for tips on that, as are the briefings mentioned above from the Mental Health Foundation and Mind. It probably comes as little surprise that processed, fried and refined foods (including refined carbohydrates), caffeine and alcohol (more on that later) and high-fat dairy are not good for our mood and are associated with increased anxiety and depression, and cutting out entire food groups is also detrimental to our mental health. This is because poor nutrition (unhealthy eating *and* unhealthy eating patterns) imbalances a whole raft of important things in our bodies, such as our blood sugar as well as the essential nutrients that our bodies and brains need to function healthily (and remember, our brains produce the 'happy hormones' we need to feel emotionally well). Again, it likely comes as no surprise as to what constitutes 'mood boosting' foods: fruits and vegetables; fish (particularly oily fish); unrefined carbohydrates; limited salt and sugar; nuts, grains and pulses; and lean meat. Oh, and don't forget water – the giver and sustainer of life! Gut health is also really important and there is a fair amount of evidence linking gut health with brain health as the brain and the gastrointestinal system is closely connected. It's no coincidence that if you go to see your doctor with a gut related issue often the first question is about stress and mood. IBS, for example, may be triggered by the immune system which is impacted by stress levels and the presence of IBS is positively associated with higher level of psychological issues, such as anxiety and depression. Following a healthy diet helps to improve gut health and may improve your well-being and, conversely, looking after your mental health can improve your gut health. So, try and get enough sleep and reduce stress if you can. There are other ways of looking after your gut, such as taking prebiotics or probiotics, drinking more water, and eating slower and better. Consuming aloe vera has also been shown to improve digestive issues.

Not only is a poor diet bad for our well-being, we can also have nutritional deficiencies which can also impact upon our mental health (and our physical health). In the UK diet there are some common deficiencies that can lead to issues that may impact your well-being: iron (causes fatigue); calcium (can cause insomnia); vitamin D (causes fatigue and mood swings); folic acid (causes fatigue and lethargy); iodine (causes tiredness); magnesium (causes loss of appetite, fatigue and insomnia); omega-3 fats (can cause fatigue, trouble sleeping, difficulties with concentration and memory); and fibre (causes tiredness). Just because they are fairly common deficiencies, this doesn't mean you are deficient as all the symptoms I've mentioned can be symptoms of a great many things so I'm not suggesting you rush out and get bottles and bottles of supplements. However, out of all of these potential nutrient deficiencies, vitamin D is a common one for those who live in the northern hemisphere, especially in the UK. The NHS advise that due to a lack of sunlight in autumn and winter (from end of September to the start of April), we should take a vitamin D supplement as our bodies won't create enough due to lack of skin exposure to sunlight. In fact, as a consequence of the pandemic stay at home order, public health officials in the UK have advised that *all* adults should take 10 micrograms of vitamin D from October to March and consider taking this throughout the year if they are not getting outdoors as much due to lockdown. So, if you're thinking of investing in any supplements, vitamin D should be on that list. If you think you're deficient in any other nutrients arrange to get a nutrient/deficiency test (there are plenty of at home one's) and, if you're particularly worried about any symptoms, speak to your GP as you may need more detailed blood analysis and other investigations. And you should always check with your GP before you start taking supplements to check that they're okay, particularly if you're taking other medications as there may be contraindications that you're unaware of.

Most people, when they decide to change their diet, do it for the physical health benefits and/or aesthetic reasons (e.g. to look better, or what they *perceive* as better) and often either aren't aware of the mental health benefits of eating well or that isn't a motivating factor behind their decision. Like exercise, though, we should do what is right for our well-being – mental and physical. And, much like moving our bodies, if we don't eat right then we don't feel right and if we don't feel right we're not motivated to eat right. And off we go on the same cyclical pattern, again and again and again. I don't know about you but when I've not eaten right I feel sluggish, tired, bloated and generally pretty shit. But, by turning why we eat well on its head and looking at it through a well-being lens rather than a physical health lens, we're much more likely to stick to eating healthily. This stands true for those who want to eat well for the physical health benefits too, as we can't truly be physically healthy until we're mentally healthy. I'm not going to say too much about this as it's the same reasoning behind why we should exercise for our mental health rather than our physical health. We just need to appreciate the mental health benefits of eating healthy and re-frame how we think about our eating habits.

I know how hard it is to motivate yourself to eat well when you're feeling emotionally all over the place. This past year has also thrown us out of our routines and has made it very easy to miss meals or eat differently than we would normally. I have been very guilty of this and it's something I'm consciously working on. I don't have any great advice beyond what you probably already know, but I'll just highlight a few things that if you can get into the habit of might give you the wee boost you need to develop heathier eating habits: drink enough water (or sparkling water or fruit tea); drink hot water with lemon; avoid caffeine after 2pm; don't skip meals (especially breakfast); eat at regular times (there's that pesky routine thing coming up again!); cook from scratch (soups and salads are great); avoid processed foods; eat the rainbow (basically eat lots of different colours of foods – but not processed foods!); eat enough fruit and vegetables; keep a bag of mixed plain nuts and raisins in the cupboard for nibbling on when you're peckish; and try and have two meat free days a week and two days where you have fish. I try to keep foods that aren't healthy out of the house (because if they're there then I'll eat them and if they're not I can't!) but I sometimes have them for the kids so I make sure to buy things that they like but I don't. Oh, and don't forget to keep some sweet treats around – I keep Skyr yoghurt and dark chocolate in the house for when I'm in the mood for something sweet. Thankfully I've not got a huge sweet tooth but I could devour a block of cheese no problem so I have to be careful with that.

There are a lot of factors that impact on your diet that aren't specifically about what you consume. For example, I find that if I plan in advance then I tend to eat healthier and am less likely to impulse buy crap when I'm doing my food shopping – meal planning is your friend! Also, getting enough sleep and exercise is important for your metabolism and motivation to eat well. Anyway, that's enough of that. Just remember the mantra: eat well to feel well.

DITCH THE BOOZE

Alcohol is often described as the 'UK's favourite coping mechanism' as we drink to alleviate stress, anxiety and a whole myriad of other mental health conditions. Most of us know it's no good for us, and certainly isn't a good coping mechanism, but jeez it can be hard to give up drinking during times of stress and anxiety. But, as outlined in the Mental Health Foundation's report *'Cheers? Understanding the relationship between alcohol and mental health'*, it's a double-edged sword: we drink to relieve stress, tension and anxiety but drinking increases symptoms of stress, tension and anxiety (and other mental health issues) and adversely affects sleep. Despite the initial stress-relieving and euphoric properties of alcohol these effects will soon wear off and often leave us feeling more depressed, anxious, stressed, worried and tired (not to mention the physical effects of a hangover). In fact, dual diagnosis of addiction and mental ill-health is incredibly common. I'm not going to go into this too much but a quick Google search will highlight hundreds upon hundreds of guides and studies which delve deeper into the link.

As someone who has struggled with mental ill-health and using alcohol as a coping mechanism, I had a gut feeling at the start of all of this back in March 2020 that alcohol use would soar during the pandemic and lockdown: the pandemic brought uncertainty and anxiety; the lockdown boredom, social isolation and loneliness. Coupled with the additional pressures of working from home, home schooling, being with your family 24/7, job loss, financial issues and lack of structure and routine and it was a recipe for disaster.

In the UK retail sales at the end of March 2020 showed a 50% increase in alcohol purchases, now this could've been due to an increase in drinking at that specific point in time or a stockpiling of alcohol for lockdown but whatever the reason, people obviously felt the need to buy more alcohol – I know I did. Regardless of why, that's a worrying increase. We were confronted with odd and conflicting messaging during lockdown – the World Health Organisation telling us not to use alcohol to cope yet the UK and Scottish Government's deeming off-licences 'essential retailers' that could remain open for business alongside food shops and pharmacies. Now, there must've been a reason for this – perhaps alcohol taxation was part of it, but Scotland, with some of the harshest alcohol policies in the UK, kept alcohol available whilst acknowledging the harms. We'll never know the reasoning behind this decision but I wonder whether there was an underlying reason this decision was taken that we don't know about; could it have been to do with the potential impact of widespread forced alcohol withdrawal on an already stretched NHS during COVID-19?

It's of little surprise that alcohol consumption has shot up exponentially in the past year, all whilst drug and alcohol support services have seen decreases in funding and access to services being severely curtailed due to lockdown. Worryingly, the drug, alcohol and mental health charity We Are With You reported a drop in referrals in April 2020 of 72%

compared to January; despite the increase in alcohol sales. In their written evidence to the Commission on Alcohol Harm: An Inquiry Into The Effects of Alcohol on Society (which reported in September 2020), the Alcohol Health Alliance UK stress that a YouGov survey reported 60% of people were less likely to seek help for non-emergency problems and Action on Addiction found that 39% of adults said they thought it would be difficult to access support and treatment for addiction during lockdown. Why? These are just informed guesses but I'd hazard a guess that people are scared of catching COVID-19 if they do go into hospital, that the high-profile redeployment of NHS staff to the front-line fight against COVID means other services are not being routinely offered, or that people are heeding the public health advice a little too rigorously and are not accessing medical treatment for fear of overwhelming the NHS. All completely understandable reasons, but mean that people are not getting help for alcohol issues until crisis point and perhaps delaying treatment until such a point that there is no way to reverse the harm that has been caused.

I've come across many stories of people who've become alcohol dependent during lockdown, and I suspect this will only be the very tip of a very large iceberg. The British Liver Trust reported a 500% increase in calls to its helpline between March and October 2020 and in April 2020, Alcohol Change UK saw a 242% rise in visits to the advice and support sections of their website. Research commissioned by Alcohol Change UK in April 2020 found that 28% of people agreed they had drunk more alcohol than normal since lockdown started and one in five reported drinking to deal with the stress and anxiety of the pandemic. A study by the University of Cambridge in May 2020 reported even higher figures, with 36% reporting an increase in alcohol consumption. This is a real concern amongst doctors, which has been outlined in a report from the Office of National Statistics; *Drinking alone: COVID-19, lockdown and alcohol-*

related harm'. Scotland – as I'm sure is the case in many other countries across the world – has seen an increase in emergency hospital admissions for alcohol related liver disease during 2020/21 (the exact figures won't be released until autumn 2021) but this increase in dangerous drinking and the decrease in seeking medical help would suggest we're going to see quite an increase. If I were a betting girl I'd put my home on it.

And what of those who were alcohol dependent prior to the pandemic? Well, lockdown was the absolute worst thing that could've happened – it was the perfect excuse to withdraw from support. And this doesn't just go for those with alcohol issues, it's the same for those with mental ill-health; lockdown removed all the barriers to withdrawing from social life and from others. No more excuses were needed; no people to see, no places to be. I can only imagine the feeling; all of the support mechanisms gone, connections gone. A survey by Action on Addiction – *'Getting in early, supporting families, and stopping the stigma of addiction'* – found that 39% of those who were in recovery reported a relapse during lockdown. And really, is it any wonder? The public purse focused on COVID-19, services were provided at a distance (and if I know anything it's that those with addictions are damn good at hiding it, especially remotely!) and people were isolated, bored, stressed, anxious and just generally feeling as 'meh' as the rest of us. What did we expect would happen? We all know that a virtual catch up with our mates wasn't the same as a proper catch up in person, did we expect any different for virtual AA meetings, for example?

I can tell you from firsthand experience that using alcohol to self-medicate is not a good idea, although I'm pretty sure most of you are already aware of that as I suspect I'm not alone in this bad habit. I know from speaking to friends and family during lockdown that they too had struggled with alcohol consumption and I've read many news articles to the same effect. One particularly jumped out at me, by Lauren O'Neill in The Guardian in January 2021, that I think summed up many people's attitudes to drinking over the past year:

> *"….I found myself steadily drinking more during the first lockdown. Pouring a drink at 6pm became one of the few ways to punctuate time, a method of marking the transition from day to evening when the only place you've been is your bedroom. Lockdown is brain-meltingly boring: the days just sit on top of one another, stale and unmoving, like oil on water. Drinking makes you feel as if something is happening – like time is moving. And it's better than another puzzle or Zoom quiz."*

I know I can't be the only one that relates to this. The problem with alcohol is that its legality deceives us somewhat into thinking it's not as bad for you as other drugs, which is simply untrue; in fact, because of its legality, it's even more damaging to public health. So, if we know it's bad for us, how can we reduce our alcohol consumption, particularly in times of high stress, anxiety and loneliness?

Firstly, I want to say that if you think you have a problem with alcohol you should always consult your GP for support as stopping 'cold turkey' can be dangerous. Secondly, you need to acknowledge that there is some form of dependency and make a plan to address the root cause of this as well as a plan for reducing your consumption. And finally, I urge you to confide in close friends and/or family – people who won't judge you and you can be honest with. I'm not here to tell you how to do any of that, there's plenty of books and support services out there to do that: AA, SMART meetings, drug and alcohol services and so forth. All I can really do is give you some pointers as to how I keep my alcohol consumption in check (or, how I reduce it when I feel it's creeping up) – and you don't have to be an 'alcoholic' (for want of a better word) to cut back on drinking, if alcohol is negatively impacting your life in any way then it may be time to think about limiting your intake.

Nothing I tell you here is a secret, it's advice that's been around forever so I'll get it over with quick: try to have two alcohol free days per week (ideally together); stick to drinking within recommended limits (in the UK the Chief Medical Officers guidelines for men *and* women is a maximum of 14 units per week, spread evenly over three days a week); drink a soft drink in between each alcoholic drink; make sure you eat properly if you're drinking; keep alcohol out of the house; keep note of how much you're drinking (there's plenty of apps out there for this); and identify your triggers for drinking (it could be that 6pm drink after work, that 8pm glass when the kids are in bed or that bottle of something cold on a hot summers day) and either avoid them (a bit of a challenge during lockdown when we're all stuck home!) or create a new routine to fill the time. See, I told you that you knew this stuff already.

One thing I find particularly helpful (on top of all the above, although I've never been particularly good at limiting my consumption – I'm an all or nothing kind of girl in most areas of my life) include tasty 'grown up' cordials and sparkling water, refreshing tonics, kombucha (which is also very good for the gut, if you can stand the vinegar taste!) and some of the alcohol-free alternatives out there. I've come to realise I like the ritual of a nice drink in a nice glass and so I now have this, but sans alcohol. There are numerous alcohol-free lagers, ciders and wine's (and let's not forget Nosecco for those special fizz-demanding occasions!) but there's an increasing number of alcohol-free spirit alternatives which are widely available online and/or in supermarkets. There are so many botanical options out there it's actually becoming a bit of a minefield, here's just some of the one's I know about and/or have tried: Ceder's; Stryyk; Celtic Soul; Lyre's; Bowser; Caleño; Three Spirit; Salcombe Distilling Co; Seedlip; Fluère; Pentire; Kolibri; Everleaf; Borrago; ZEO; Crossip; Feragaia; Nonsuch; Wilfred's; Clean Co; Mother Root; Warner's…I could go on and I'm sure I've missed some out, but I won't. And some of them are delicious. Forewarning through, they're expensive (often more expensive than their alcoholic counterparts) because the distilling process is more complicated. Nevertheless, I don't drink nearly as much of these drinks as I do alcoholic spirits because I drink to enjoy the flavour rather than drink for the alcohol high (not that I don't drink alcohol for the taste too, but let's be honest, the 'buzz' is also a factor) so they last a lot longer. In fact, even traditional alcohol manufacturers are starting to recognise the trend in alcohol-free alternatives and the potential to increase their profits and are beginning their foray into alcohol-free spirits (such as Gordon's) and I suspect that more and more manufacturers and drink companies will catch on.

I can't really give advice beyond what's already out there. Cutting back on alcohol – or stopping altogether – is not easy if you are either dependent or reliant on it. You need to find what works for you and that will vary from person to person. But reach out for support if you need it, take up a new hobby to fill your time, introduce more self-care into your routine and think about all that money you'll save as well as how much better you'll feel – physically and mentally. Giving up or cutting back on the booze (or any other substance) is, without doubt, the best thing you can do for your mental health and well-being. Try it, you won't be disappointed.

SLEEP WELL

Sleep is as important to the human body as water and food. Our bodies cannot survive without sleep and sleep is essential to our physical health, growth, and recovery from illness. There's a reason why, when we are sick, that we feel tired and need more sleep; our bodies need to conserve energy to enable our immune system to fight infection. Notwithstanding the physical benefits, without at least seven hours of good quality sleep we may also start to experience issues with our cognitive and behavioural functioning as our brains struggle, such as delayed reaction, lapses in attention, fatigue, hallucinations and mood swings; which will only get worse the less sleep we have. Anyone who's ever struggled with insomnia or those who've had children can vouch for the impact of lack of good quality sleep.

Lack of sleep isn't just associated with poor physical health but also with poor mental health. Harvard Medical School highlight the link between sleep and poor mental health, stating that chronic sleep issues affect between 50% to 80% of those in a typical psychiatric practice, in comparison to between 10% to 18% of those in the general population in the US. They go on to explain that studies have found that between 65% and 90% of adults with severe depression are likely to experience problems with sleep, 50% of those with some form of generalised anxiety are likely to have sleep issues and 69% to 99% of those with bipolar disorder are likely to experience insomnia or sleep less during a manic episode. Furthermore, problems with sleep is likely to increase your risk of developing particular mental health conditions, such as anxiety and depression and, on the flip side of the coin, those with poor mental health are more likely to experience insomnia and other sleep issues (such as sleep apnea, narcolepsy and restless legs syndrome). So, much like alcohol, there is a two-way relationship between sleep and mental health and well-being which only makes it more important to address our sleeping habits, particularly at times of high stress and anxiety. The problem with sleep deprivation is that the evidence suggests that your body can develop a tolerance to it, leading to chronic sleep deprivation. Therefore, even though you may be struggling with lack of sleep you may not even be aware of it as this has become your status quo. This is a dangerous place to be, both physically and mentally. Sleep hygiene, therefore, is incredibly important.

We all have an internal body clock which is known as our circadian rhythm; a 24-hour clock which makes us become increasingly tired after we wake up. As explained by the Sleep Foundation, there are four stages to sleep; and we need to get enough of the stage of sleep in which our heartbeat, breathing and brain wave activity reach their lowest levels for us to feel properly rested when we wake.

The amount of sleep we need varies with age, but adults between aged 18 to 64-years need between seven and nine hours per day. However, our circadian rhythm is affected by a number of things, including natural things such as light and noise but also what we drink, the food we eat and the electronic devices we use.

Depending on where you live in the world, you may struggle with some external factors more than others, in particular light. Certain areas of the world experience 24-hour days and 24-hour nights depending upon the time of year and this can play havoc to your circadian rhythm. Living in Scotland I can relate to the struggle that occurs when the seasons and hours of daylight change, especially with the kids who think bedtime is only 'when it's dark outside'. In December 2019, I took my boys to Luosto in Finnish Lapland to do all things

Christmas and I have honestly never experienced anything quite like Polar Night in the Arctic Circle. The sun rose (but not above the horizon) at around 11.30am and set again before 1pm. It was the strangest thing going to bed and getting up in the dark, eating breakfast and dinner in the dark and doing your activities in the dark, with just a short slightly brighter (although never proper 'daylight') reprieve for an hour or so at lunch time. And, of course, in summer the sun doesn't set in the Arctic Circle as they experience the Midnight Sun (with the reverse being true in the Antarctic Circle). Now, I only experienced Polar Night for four days and my body clock was all over the place; I have never been so glad to get back to the seven or so hours of winter daylight in Scotland. This experience really hit home how important our circadian rhythm is and I'm not embarrassed to admit that the lack of daylight – even for those four days – really affected my mood (had it not been for all the sledging, snowmobiling, amethyst mining and husky sledding I probably would've been a right pain in the arse!). So yeah, be aware of the impact of external factors on your sleep and try and find a way to tackle this; make use of blackout blinds and curtains or noise-cancelling headphones or ear plugs.

Most of poor sleep hygiene (with the exception of light and noise) is self-inflicted and entirely within our own gift to change. I admit I am pretty rubbish with this – before lockdown I was in my bed early and up early, now…not so much. I'm lucky these days if I get to bed before 2am. But, as with much of the advice in this chapter, I aspire to do better! I know what to do to improve my sleep, in particular setting regular bedtime and getting up hours, but it's hard with the lack of structure (note to self: go back to 'routine' and take note!). Although I rarely watch TV in my bedroom, I am guilty of perusing the internet, social media and playing mindless games on my phone; something which I know is not good for my sleep and endeavor to do less of! I do my utmost to avoid caffeine after 2pm (although I do cram it in before then), you should also avoid alcohol (which I have varying levels of success with) and I know that big meals and eating certain foods (such as chocolate, cheese, spicy and sweet foods) in the hours before bedtime isn't a good idea. I do, however, make sure my bedroom is kept at a comfortable temperature with fresh air circulating (I like my bedroom to be cool and well ventilated, but you may be different so find what works for you temperature-wise) and I try and keep lighting low. These are the obvious things that most people think about when we talk about improving our sleeping habits.

There are some others, which are very specific to each of us. I have a lovely aroma diffuser in my room that I put on before I go to bed with lavender and/or chamomile to help me sleep (also good for headaches). I also like to have a lovely warm bubble bath before bed, ideally with candles and a good book. I like reading (although nothing too serious) before bed as it switches my brain off from all the external pressures and mounting 'to do' lists. And as a special treat I love nothing more than some super comfy pyjamas and freshly washed bed linen, especially if it's been hung outside to dry!

This hasn't always been the case but as I've got older, and having had some amazing nights' sleep in hotels, I decided to invest in a great night's sleep at home. I bought a luxurious bed, a medium-firm mattress (after trying out lots of different ones!), a memory foam mattress topper, goose down pillows and duvet (I'm not a fan of synthetic duvets), satin pillowcases, and Egyptian cotton bed linen (and fleece and/or brushed cotton for the winter). I also have some lovely soft throws and blankets for those extra cold nights (I do love a bit of hygge). Given I spend the majority of my life in my bed I think it's probably the best investment I've ever made. Sometimes, when I've got a headache or am feeling particularly stressed or anxious I wear a heated eye mask (with a timer so it switches off if I fall asleep). And most nights I listen to the rain or ocean sounds to help lull me to sleep. Thankfully, I'm not bothered by noise, but I have friends who swear by ear plugs.

So, what's best for you to improve your sleep is something you need to figure out. But figure it out, make some changes and you'll start to sleep like a baby and you'll feel better for it too.

FIND A CREATIVE OUTLET

Yes, it's true – creativity has numerous benefits for your well-being. It provides you with time for yourself, an opportunity to meet (or in COVID times, virtually meet) new people, a break from worry and stress, a healthy coping mechanism and it can improve your health. When you're being creative, you are focused entirely on what you're doing so your mind isn't worrying over things that have happened or could happen, or what someone said or did or what you said or did. Creativity is almost like a type of meditation as it brings complete mindfulness (more on that later) and also a sense of accomplishment (which releases dopamine, the body's natural anti-depressant). Furthermore, not only does creativity distract the mind, but a creative outlet can enable you to express feelings that you otherwise may not voice; it can be an outlet for your emotions and help you to make sense of your experiences.

Doing an activity you enjoy has numerous health benefits, such as; lowering cortisol (the stress hormone) and blood pressure, boosting your immune system, reduced BMI, and reduced anxiety and depression. Furthermore, creativity has also been linked to improved brain function and a reduction in symptoms associated with dementia. A study in San

Francisco even found that work performance is increased by creativity as you become more innovative, collaborative and more of a team player. A 2010 article, *'The Connection between Art, Healing and Public Health: A Review of Current Literature'*, in the American Journal of Public Health found a positive link between engaging in the creative arts (music, visual arts, movement-based creative expression and expressive writing) and physical and mental health outcomes. It should come as little surprise that therapeutic arts and creative therapies are becoming more and more popular for treatment for mental ill-health – such as dance movement therapy, music therapy, visual arts therapy, amongst others – particularly for children, those unable to communicate verbally and those dealing with clinical issues in the subconscious (such as significant 'buried' trauma).

Whether you use art to deal with an underlying mental health issue, or simply as a stress relieving tool does not matter. The fact remains that creativity is good for you.

You may not think you have a creative bone in your body, but I challenge everyone to try and find something you enjoy. When I say creative it doesn't have to mean whipping out the canvas and watercolours or clay to start that sculpture; creativity comes in all shapes and sizes. Baking, cooking, drawing, calligraphy, dancing, playing a musical instrument, gardening, sewing, colouring, crochet, painting, knitting, writing, pottery, personal style; interior design; basically, anything that uses your imagination is creative.

Despite my B in Higher Art & Design, I am utterly rubbish at arts and crafts and I'm embarrassed to say that I still get my mum to do my sewing for me. But I do have other creative outlets that I enjoy. I love to write, fiction and non-fiction. I love to cook (it's often said that I can never make the same dish the same way twice as I never measure or weigh ingredients). I love interior design and can spend hours researching and planning what each room in my house will look like when I'm done. And, it seems obvious now, but until right now I hadn't realised that cooking and decorating my home *were* creative outlets.

Creativity soothes the soul and quietens the mind and there is nothing quite like it when you're feeling overwhelmed. I can't think of how I'd have coped during the past year without my writing and I know I'm not alone; this book is full of stories where people used creativity to pass time and help them manage stress. Writing has brought me so much peace and calm in an otherwise chaotic, unpredictable and stressful time. The theory of cognition asserts that creativity is the basis of human life and I can't think of a better reason – beyond that it makes you feel bloody good – to find something creative to enjoy.

Those who have fared better throughout COVD-19 have undoubtedly done so as a result of their positive coping mechanisms. Whilst it might seem like a herculean effort to set a routine, go to bed and get up early, eat well, exercise more, go outside and find a creative hobby that distracts you when you're feeling utterly shit, taking these small steps is exactly how you will start to feel better. And, as you start to feel better, you'll have the ability to do more and focus on building your resilience for life's future troughs.

LESSONS IN RESILIENCE

You've probably heard lots of talk about resilience, but what does it actually mean? I consider myself fairly emotionally literate but until I actually started doing research for this book I hadn't really thought much about what resilience actually was or what it entailed. Yes, I knew what the benefits were and I had my own theories and ideas as to what resilience was, but it was very enlightening reading about it and I've certainly learnt some lessons on how to improve my own resilience.

So, what is resilience? Fundamentally it's our ability to emotionally cope with life stress, and the length of time it takes us to recover from those stresses is directly linked to how psychologically resilient we are. Take a physical stress on your body, for example. The healthier your body is, the easier it can deal with it and the quicker it can recover from stress (such as illness or even pregnancy). The mind is the same. The healthier and, therefore, more resilient it is, the easier it will find stress to deal with and the faster it will bounce back. This is resilience. And it's as important to be mentally resilient as it is for your body to be physically resilient. If you don't have resilience your mental health and overall well-being (including your physical well-being) will suffer. You need a healthy body *and* a healthy mind to flourish in life. So, ignore your mental health at your peril because I'm afraid you can't avoid pressure and stress in life.

Human development expert, Dr Kenneth Ginsburg, proposes seven components of resilience – known as the seven c's – all of which are interdependent: competence; confidence, connection; character; contribution; coping; and control. There are many different models of resilience out there, Dr Ginsburg's being one, but I prefer one from The Bounce Back Project: Promoting Health through Happiness (a collaboration of physicians, nurses, healthcare leaders and community members focusing on promoting emotional, mental and physical health through happiness) as it's simpler and I feel it fits better with contemporary adult life. It suggests five pillars to resilience (which can be mapped against the seven c's): self-care; self-awareness; relationships; mindfulness; and purpose. You need all of them to be optimally resilient. If you Google it you'll find all sorts of colourful diagrams showing how the overlap of these five pillars (or skills if you'd rather call them that) are essential for optimum resilience. And the chances are that you'll be better at some parts than others (I, for example, am utterly crap at being mindful – I try, and I love a bit of mindfulness meditation and I can see clearly the benefits of living mindfully, but can I do it? No). That's fine, it just means you need to practice some of the pillars more than others.

As I've said, life stress is normal. In fact, stress can actually be a good thing; it can motivate us, propel us forward and even make us more efficient (I find a healthy dose of stress is needed for me to meet deadlines, for example). Stress (at least the type of stress most of us encounter in our daily lives) in and of itself is not bad or good. It's just stress. It's our feelings toward and capacity to deal with stress that's important. There are, however, different 'types' of stress: positive stress (this is the normal stress response to a normal situation, such as a job interview); tolerable stress (the body's stress response to a more severe event, such as a bereavement, but with supportive mechanisms in place); and toxic stress (prolonged stress response to ongoing or cumulative events, such as ongoing exposure to domestic violence or even a pandemic). If you do not have resilience then tolerable stress may become difficult to bear and, in some severe cases, even positive stress may become intolerable as your mental health declines and all stress becomes toxic. It is this toxic stress which is so harmful to your well-being and, if left unchecked, may lead to long term problems with your mental, social and physical health (see the 1998 Adverse Childhood Experiences (ACE) study by the Centers for Disease Control and Prevention-Kaiser Permanente in Southern California, US for further information on toxic stress and ACE's). So, you see why building resilience becomes essential to enable you to cope with the stress that life is going to throw at you. To nab a quote from the Bounce Back Project's website:

> *"Think of it [stress] like a fire. When the fire is in the fireplace, it is beautiful and relaxing, and in the winter it keeps one warm. But if the fire gets out of control, it can burn down the house. The fire is neither good nor bad, it just exists. It is how the fire is contained or controlled that determines whether it is going to have a beneficial or harmful effect…Stress is unavoidable; it is how well we manage and respond to our stress that really determines if it is going to have an adverse or beneficial effect in our lives."*

So, it's better to keep our fires in the fireplace than allowing it to burn our whole house down. That, my friend, is resilience.

Resilience isn't something we're born with, it's not in our DNA; it's something we have to learn and practice – consistency is essential if you want to become resilient. You can't just become resilient by doing something once, it takes work and commitment. The more often you act, the more you'll develop your ability. It doesn't matter where you start on the resilience spectrum, you can always improve. Take small steps or huge leaps, whatever works for you, and so long as you're doing *something* you'll reap the benefits in terms of your resilience.

THE BENEFITS OF SELF-CARE

Self-care is essential at all times, but particularly so during times of high stress and anxiety. Sometimes people think putting yourself first is selfish but it is far from it. If you've ever flown before you'll be familiar with the phrase 'put your own mask on before helping others'. Simply put, you can't help anyone else if you burn out yourself. Self-care is about making sure we can function, even in the midst of the stress and challenges of modern life, and to do so with confidence, enthusiasm and strength.

Self-care encompasses many things, most of which I've already discussed as coping strategies (I talk about them separately to highlight the importance of those specific actions as ways to help structure your life in a healthier way) but consider them all overlapping self-care strategies to promote good mental health and well-being at any time. Whilst the actions I've already spoken about are things you can do in times of high stress when you're struggling to cope to make yourself feel better, they are also things you should do all the time to increase your resilience to trauma and life stress so you don't get overwhelmed in the first place. Better to be proactive than reactive, after all!

The one very important thing about self-care is that it's not passive; it requires you to identify and initiate action. It relies on self-awareness (more on that next) and your active engagement to make it happen. Think of it like any goal you might have in life – you won't achieve it if you don't work towards it. You are in control and it is up to you to take the steps to make it happen. Self-care is work, but it should be fun work.

So what else do we mean by self-care? There is no definitive list *per se*, rather it's about doing what you need to do to look after yourself physically, emotionally and mentally. Self-care means different things and is unique to each person. What may help me may not help you (I like to write, for example, but to you that might seem like a boring almighty chore!). Some aspects of self-care are universal and are physiological (such as eating well, exercising, avoiding drugs and alcohol and so forth), but other methods of self-care are person-specific and the world is your oyster!

Self-care really is just about looking after yourself in a way that makes *you* feel good. I have many different things I like to do to look after my emotional health through self-care: I like a good TV series or movie with a face mask and a cup of tea; I love cooking a new meal from scratch; I like a bubble bath with a good book; I love being out in the middle of a loch on the paddle board; and a nice scented candle or a bunch of flowers always makes me feel good. All are examples of self-care and things I enjoy. They may well be your worst nightmare. Some people enjoy tinkering away with DIY, going for a cycle or long walk, baking, or fixing their car or gardening. They're all acts of self-care if you enjoy them, they make you feel good and allow your body and mind to relax. I've signed myself up to a flower subscription service and receive a beautiful bunch of flowers every fortnight for no other reason than I love having fresh flowers in the house and they make me smile when they arrive. The joy of those flowers lasts for weeks. That's self-care – it's not about the flowers *per se*, but the feeling those flowers provide. Yes, it costs, but the social return and value of investment (the positive impact it has on me) is by far greater than the money I spend on the actual flowers.

Self-care is what makes you feel good. Lockdown has made this particularly hard as we aren't able to do some of the things that make us feel good, such as exercise classes or swimming. I don't know about you, but during Lockdown 1.0 and 2.0 I didn't put a huge amount of effort into my presentation. Don't get me wrong, I was always washed and clean and so on, but there were days I didn't get dressed because I had no reason to, and certainly no reason to dress up (I think I even attended my work virtual Christmas party in my pyjamas!). Yet sometimes I feel better when I look better so there were days when I needed a mental boost that I did my hair and put on some 'outdoor' clothes. I remember at one point during the first lockdown, before I headed out on my social outing of the week – the food shop of all places! – putting a post on social media deliberating over whether to wear *'jeans and a nice top or a dress'* for such a special occasion. As everyone related to our lack of having to get dressed and look good it attracted all manner of funny responses, in the end I was instructed that this was a full ballgown, stiletto and red lippy occasion! Although I think I just settled for jeans and a nice top. Sometimes during lockdown, I just wanted to feel 'different' and put on some tinted moisturiser and mascara. Find something that makes you feel good (it doesn't have to cost anything) – hell, it can even be as simple as shaving (face or legs!) – and try it!

A quick word of caution because sometimes harmful things feel good too. Avoid doing too much of the things that make you feel good in the short-term and only temporarily fill your bucket – shopping, drinking too much, one-night stand's with strangers (not much chance of that in the midst of lockdown!) and so on. Although that initial dopamine rush is great, it doesn't last and can contribute towards mental ill-health (not to mention addiction; there's a reason things that make you feel deliriously good in the short-term tend to be the things we get addicted to!). Apologies if I come across a bit preachy, I don't mean to be. I've fallen down the rabbit hole of making myself feel good from things that were not good and I ended up feeling totally and utterly shit. Short-term dopamine boosts tend to be quick fixes and just as putting a plaster on a broken bone wouldn't help, neither will they, not in the long term anyway.

So sometimes self-care can involve *not* doing something. Yes, it can be the things I've spoken about above that make you feel top of the world but will make you feel worse later (and, eugh, the guilt – we've all been there, my friends and I call it hangover guilt), but saying 'no' can be a powerful act of self-care. You might need peace and quiet and don't want to speak to people for a day or two – fine. You might not want to do that girls night in – fine. You might not be able to help out that friend – fine. It is absolutely a-okay to say no if you need a break. I've been very guilty of this people pleasing in the past. I like to help people and I'll bend over backwards to do it, sometimes to the detriment of my own well-being. And you know what? That is *not* okay. Not if you want to be okay yourself. And that birthday or Mother's Day or whatever day that's coming up? Guess what? You don't need to go all out for it. Not if you're at the end of your tether and it's going to stress you out. So, put yourself first and say no sometimes. Avoid burn out, because I promise you it's not fun.

Another thing I do when I need to wind down the chatter in my head and re-charge is switch off. Often, when I'm feeling overly stressed, anxious or experiencing low mood, I ignore my phone. It isn't that I'm ignoring a specific person or that I don't want to talk to particular people, but that I'm consciously putting myself in a protective bubble of peace, calm and quiet – from everyone. Sometimes the last thing I want to do is talk to people, any people, whether they are friends or family (and, dare I say it, sometimes even my kids whom I love dearly but are not always conducive to introspection and calm). I just want to sit and be alone with my thoughts or watch mind numbing TV or read a book to escape. And, you know what? That's okay. It took me a long time to accept that I was not only allowed to do it, but that I was actively looking after myself and my mental health (it took a bit of an emotional breakdown for me to realise this, so take my word for it!). Many of my friends are the same and I know if they're not answering the phone or my messages go unanswered for a few days that they're needing peace to deal with their own minds (although if it goes on for a long time I always know to check in and make sure they're okay). So, if I ignore your call I'm not being horrible or rude, I'm practicing self-care. If you need a break from the world, if all the plate spinning is becoming overwhelming and you need to switch off as I do, then don't feel bad if you shut off the outside world for a day or two to focus on yourself. And do not *ever* apologise for it.

It's a balancing act is self-care. I like the analogy my kids were taught when they first started school – everyone has a bucket that needs to be kept full, and to keep that bucket full you need to be kind to others *and* be kind to yourself. So, if you're unkind – to others or yourself, you'll empty your bucket. Self-care fills your bucket.

THE IMPORTANCE OF SELF-AWARENESS

If self-awareness sounds easy, it's not. Truly understanding yourself – your strengths and weaknesses, beliefs and morals, thoughts and feelings, passions and motivations – is both challenging and daunting. It requires you to delve into and accept parts of your personality that you are not comfortable with or may not particularly want to accept. But to genuinely understand yourself and what makes you tick is a powerful gift in self-awareness and you will come to understand how and why other people think of you the way they do, why people behave towards you in the way they do and why you respond in certain ways towards others. It's a simple matter of cause and effect and one of the first things we teach children when we say *'think about how that makes someone else feel'*. We've all heard the term *'no man is an island'* – that is what self-awareness teaches you.

There are huge benefits to really getting to know your thoughts, how this influences your character and how it impacts on others and the world around you. In essence, self-awareness acts as a stress-related performance-enhancer. Think back to some challenging times in your life and how you fared – oftentimes when you look back to times of high stress and/or pressure you'll say *'I don't know how I got through that'*. You got through it because of self-awareness, it's like psychological adrenaline, which takes us back to our surge capacity. Professor Ann Masten of the University of Minnesota explains that, as humans, we 'tune in' to our energy 'reservoir' to live in periods of high stress and key to replenishing our surge capacity is looking inwards to really consider why we feel the way we do. Yes, we need to do all the acts of self-care we've already spoken about but we also need to stop and check in with our thoughts, feelings and emotions. Only by doing this are we able to give ourselves what we really need to sustain ourselves through difficult times in life.

Let's start with the hardest bit – identifying the negative parts of yourself, your 'flaws'. You may think *'no way in hell do I want to know that'* because you're probably not going to like the answers, I know I didn't. But, like it or not, we're human and we all have flaws. However, whilst recognising the difficult behaviours, emotions, thoughts and values we hold is difficult, it is the foundation for true self-awareness. We have to be open to our own thoughts and feelings before we can truly accept the impact they have on ourselves and on others and this enables us to take action if we don't like it. Susan David, a psychologist at Harvard Medical School, has devoted her life's work to understanding emotional agility and the impact it has on our actions and decisions in life – a desire that was driven by her experience of growing up in apartheid South Africa where racism had been legislated and she saw, first-hand, the impact of people's beliefs on their actions and subsequently on the lives of others. She did a fantastic TED Talk (*'The gift and power of emotional courage'*) on emotional agility which I thoroughly recommend you watch where she explains that by identifying and labelling *"...our emotions accurately we are more able to discern the precise cause of our feelings...and what scientists call the readiness potential in our brain is activated allowing us to take concrete steps. But not just any steps, but the right steps for us. Because our emotions are data. Our emotions contain flashing lights to things that we care about."* Therefore, by properly understanding yourself you properly understand what steps you need to take to better align your actions with your values. This makes you happier, which contributes to improved resilience.

Yes, it's an uncomfortable process but it's meant to be. I've yet to find someone who has pondered their own selves and *hasn't* come out of it in tears, anger, frustration, embarrassment and/or shame. They're not in any way bad people – far from it, they are some of the most amazing people I know – but it's not easy to admit to your shortcomings. When it comes to our limitations we often play the ostrich, I know I did anyway, but what makes a well-rounded self-aware person is knowing exactly what their flaws are. Yes, it's not fun, you'll probably feel shit for a bit but at least you know. It's a bit like finally opening up your credit card statement instead of burying it at the bottom of that drawer; you can only face up to the problem when you know the full scale of it – even if it is ugly. Nevertheless, in her TED Talk, Susan David alludes to the cost of a lack of self-awareness: *"I grew up in the white suburbs of apartheid South Africa, a country and community committed to not seeing."* Apartheid South Africa is an example of the worst ultimate cost of a lack of self-awareness.

I think part of true self-awareness comes with age, reflection and experience, but it's a skill we can all learn. We know we're not perfect but it takes a brave person to admit to their flaws. When I became fully aware of some of the less desirable parts of my being I was embarrassed and ashamed – but now I make a conscious effort to try and quell those rather pesky parts of my personality it doesn't fit with my values and I don't like how they make others feel and react. I won't lie, it can be hard to change because your personality is hard-wired through upbringing and social conditioning. However, the more self-aware you are the easier it becomes; I find myself having to bite my tongue less and less, although it's still a conscious effort. But what this self-awareness has done is give me an understanding of how I can control my reactions towards others – I know I can actively choose to not say or do something in retaliation to something that is said or done to me. I don't always manage it, but I try. I scroll on by social media posts that piss me off, I unfollow people that annoy me and I actively remove myself from situations that don't bring out the best in me. That's what self-awareness has done for me and it's made me feel all the better for it. Yes, it's uncomfortable, but the benefits far outweigh this discomfort. I am way less stressed and anxious about the world around me because of this. And you can deal with all those negative emotions too, it's completely within your gift: you just need to figure out what makes you tick.

THE SIGNIFICANCE OF RELATIONSHIPS

This one is a bit of a no-brainer – positive relationships enable us to cope with adversity and bounce back from stress and trauma. The importance of positive relationships relies heavily on self-awareness insofar as you may struggle to build positive relationships if you're not aware of how your thoughts and actions impact on others or how you react to others'. Who'd want to be around someone who didn't think about the consequences of their words, for example? Not me. Whilst we're all guilty of being insensitive now and again, if you're not aware or able to apologise for it then who's going to want to hang around with you? I can be terribly intolerant and irrational at times but I have a fairly strong moral compass and will always apologise if, in hindsight, I look back and realise I was being a complete arse. So, what I can't abide is people who never admit they're wrong, never apologise and never give a second thought as to the impact of their words or behaviour on others. Those people are not self-aware and those are not people you want around you. When you think about the people in your life, I'd bet that they're all (or nearly all) people whose company you enjoy, who you connect with and with whom you probably have similar morals and values. Any relationship that isn't reciprocally supportive is toxic and the effort is often not worth the detrimental impact on your well-being (more on that later).

Love, trust and connection are essential for our emotional equilibrium so it should come as no surprise that relationships built on these foundations bolster your resilience. You need to surround yourself with people who make you feel happier, safe and fulfilled. These people will encourage you and provide reassurance when times are tough and they'll celebrate with you when times are good. 'Fair weather friends' are not friends, they're drinking buddies – they're not the people you need around you when life throws a curve ball. It's the people who stick by you when that happens, they're the real deal. Take me, for example. When I was in my early 20's I witnessed a fatal motorbike accident. It was incredibly traumatic and took me quite a bit of time to recover from the anxiety, insomnia, nightmares and panic attacks. To this day the memories still linger in my mind and cause anxiety when I'm driving. At the time one of my friends from university was studying in Germany – I hadn't known her that long nor particularly well – but she was so worried about me that she sent a friend of hers (who I knew even less) round to make sure I was okay. Needless to say, those two people are now good friends of mine. That's the kind of relationships you want in your life; the one's with the people who you can seek out when you're in trouble or need help. These are the people who, irrespective of what they're going through, will always be there for you. These relationships don't just happen (or, if they do you're incredibly lucky!), they take continued effort and understanding. But those people...they're your people and you're their people.

If you have close relationships with the people you live with during lockdown then you are doubly lucky as your hugging also helps to lower our stress and anxiety levels. Why? Well, hugging releases those happy hormones, in particular oxytocin – a hormone released into our bloodstream when we're in love (and in labour) that is responsible for social bonding (as well as reproduction, childbirth and post-natal connection). Oxytocin is often referred to as the 'cuddle hormone' and just a 20 second hug is enough to lower your blood pressure and reduce the stress hormones. So, get hugging!

Connections with other people are the most important and impactful experiences we have in our lives. Go back to any story in this book and it'll highlight the importance of the relationships in their lives, not only in helping them through the pandemic and lockdown, but also the impact of temporary loss (due to lockdown) and/or bereavement. It should come as no surprise then that the more positive supportive relationships you have in your life, the happier you'll be and the more resilient you'll be to stress. With the right people around you, dealing with the shit life throws at you will be all the much easier. So, go forth; find your tribe and nurture.

THE VALUE OF MINDFULNESS

Look up 'mindfulness' in any dictionary and you'll find a plethora of similar definitions, all with one similarity: being consciously aware of the present moment. Like being self-aware, it sounds easy; and for some it is. But some of us – me included – really struggle with being mindful. You can be mindful in feelings, thoughts and physical sensations (such as taste and texture through eating mindfully, or smells and sounds whilst on a mindful walk). To be mindful you need to be actively aware of the present, focusing your full attention on the physical sensations of the moment you're in. In guided meditation you'll be asked to 'check in' to your body by 'scanning' the sensations from head to toe. You'll then be asked to witness your thoughts from a place of slight separation with a sentence along the lines of 'as thoughts come into your mind, observe them and let them pass without judgement'. If you can master this, you are being mindful, living right there and then with no thought to the outside, just your physical presence.

In being mindful, your focus on the present results in your being more involved and enriched by the experiences you are having. You've probably all heard the saying 'put away the camera and enjoy the experience'; I guess mindfulness is the same thing (although I do love a photo!). Put simply, it's about living in the moment rather than worrying about the past or stressing about the future. Being mindful doesn't mean we don't have negative thoughts or feelings. We do, that again is part of the human condition. But, by living mindfully, we acknowledge that those thoughts and feelings exist but we don't dwell on them. The theory is – and it works, on the few occasions I've managed it – that by doing this we stop our thought process from taking over our sense of self to enable us to identify negative thought patterns and keep control of our perception of the outside world. So, the goal of mindfulness is not to control your thoughts. The very opposite in fact. The goal of mindfulness is to stop your thoughts from controlling you.

Before I discuss the mental health benefits of mindfulness, I'll quickly highlight some of the many physical benefits of adopting the practice. Many studies have been conducted on the physical health benefits of mindfulness, including on: heart disease; high blood pressure; poor sleep; gastrointestinal issues; chronic pain; focus and attention span; pain tolerance; memory loss; and addictions. I recently attended a webinar on social justice hosted by Community Justice Scotland where Sir Harry Burns (Professor of Global Public Health at the University of Strathclyde and former Chief Medical Officer for Scotland) was speaking with the other panelists about how we can improve health inequalities, particularly in light of COVID-19 and he mentioned mindfulness and emphasised that mindfulness and meditation actually changes the way the brain functions as it improves blood flow to the brain. Now, I don't know about you, but I think that's remarkable and even if you don't believe in the mental health benefits, if you practice meditation or mindfulness for nothing else but the physical benefits then you're going to benefit. Plus, it's free and you can do it anywhere. Even without the mental health benefits, I'm sold!

We're all human and we all worry and stress over things. I know I do. Even things I don't need to worry and stress over. Living this way has been ingrained into us in the way we live our lives today. Worry, worry, worry, Stress, stress, stress. It's almost become a competition – the more stressed you are, the more successful you are. Well, bollocks to that. What complete and utter shite. Don't get me wrong, I lived that way too and I still fall foul of it every now and then. But, after a fairly significant breakdown I realised that it was time to stop worrying about things from my past or things that might happen in my future – and my life wasn't even that stressful. I can only imagine how people feel who have more plates to spin and more to lose if they drop them. My pressure was largely self-inflicted; pressure I put on myself to be who everyone else wanted me to be, or at least who I thought I should be. So, one messy shit-show later and I know how important it is to try not to worry or fixate on things that have already happened or that I cannot control, in particular things that may or may not happen in future.

You'll have seen many quotes to the effect of 'life is not a dress rehearsal', 'live each day as if it were your last' and 'tomorrow isn't guaranteed', amongst others. These are all essentially calls to be mindful; to live in the present. As always, the Dalai Lama is way more eloquent:

> *"There are only two days in the year that nothing can be done. One is called Yesterday and the other is called Tomorrow. Today is the right day to Love, Believe, Do and mostly Live."*

Aye, he's a very wise man indeed. It's probably no surprise that mindfulness traces its roots back to Buddhism as a way to aid the journey to enlightenment by becoming less egotistical and reaching a state of 'no self' which will ultimately (or at least hopefully) lead to nirvana. What we've come to know as mindfulness in the western world has somewhat lost its eastern roots, but Buddhists still practice 'samma sati' (right mindfulness) as part of the Buddha's Eightfold Path to enlightenment.

Buddhism has some fascinating teachings on being mindful and I'd urge you to read them. I was lucky enough to spend some time at Kagyu Samye Ling Monastery in Eskdalemuir (I know, right, a Buddhist Temple in Scotland, whatever next?) when I was studying religious studies, and even as a surly hormonal teenager I was appreciative of its serenity, even getting up at 6am to participate in the Tara Prayers alongside the nuns and monks. There was a complete feeling of peacefulness and calm. That was a long time ago now, right enough, but to this day I'd love to go back and, one day even take my children. I think now, 23 years later with life experience under my belt, I'd appreciate it all the more (it was a tad wasted on a bunch of 16-year-olds!). The closest I think I've ever come to the sense of calm I felt meditating and praying at Samye Ling has been the sleepy peacefulness after a sound bath or the calm euphoria of smoke saunas and ice swimming in Finland. As I write this in March 2021, stuck at home almost a year after the first lockdown, I feel an almost physical pull to go back to Samye Ling, or at least have a sauna or sound bath! Mindful meditation on my own doesn't quite work for me, you see, I need prompting and guidance.

There are lots of way you can practice mindfulness. You can do a mindfulness meditation – there are loads online and many apps which you can download with guided meditations. There are mindful activities, such as jigsaws, reading or colouring in. Anything you do that enables you to focus on the now and be completely present is mindful. It doesn't have to be meditation (although I thoroughly recommend it because if you can master the technique of observing thoughts it is utterly blissful), it can literally be anything that focuses your mind and attention on the present to stop you ruminating on the past or stressing over the future.

Psychotherapist Esther Emmanuel gave advice in an article for Happiful magazine in October 2020 on how to replenish our surge capacity through mindful techniques: when you wake up take it slowly and quietly and pay attention to your thoughts and feelings; play soothing music or have a bath and be aware of the sounds and feelings; and learn how to just 'be' in the moment and let your worries go for as long as you can. By doing this, and being more mindful, you will decrease stress, anxiety and depression and enable you to better regulate your emotions. All good things if you want to be more resilient to life's pressures.

Now, go get yourself some zen.

THE POWER OF PURPOSE

We've already spoken about the importance of self-awareness, and one of the benefits of self-awareness is in better understanding your 'purpose'. You'll have no doubt heard a lot of talk about finding 'purpose' in your life and its benefits, and that's all well and good, but what do we actually mean when we talk about finding purpose and again, why is it important?

Purpose is the appreciation and understanding that there is something bigger in the world than just ourselves and that we have something to give to this world, something beyond our own lives and our immediate existence. You can find purpose in lots of things and it's likely that whatever this purpose is, is probably a large part of your identity. Your purpose – whatever it may be – is what shapes our thinking, beliefs and attitudes towards others and the world around us. For example, you may find purpose in religion or vocation or politics. You may have heard other people talk about your purpose as your 'why'. It's often made to sound complicated but it's really not. It's the reason you get out of bed every day. It's the reason that you feel excited and passionate and satisfied.

I find the work of the German philosopher, Friedrich Nietzsche helpful when thinking about and understanding what we mean by 'purpose'. Nietzsche spent his life trying to understand the motivations that underpinned nineteenth century Western ideology, seeking to understand what drove people to believe the things they did; he wanted to understand human motivation. But people struggled with his work, labelling him a 'nihilist' as he believed that traditional values and beliefs were largely unfounded and that human existence was intrinsically senseless and purposeless. He believed that in order to give some sense to their existence, people filled it with belief systems that gave them purpose – such as religion. This was fundamental to the development of existentialism: the belief that our existence is essentially meaningless and that it's solely the responsibility of the individual to give purpose to life and that it's for us and us alone to decide what this is. Our lives are, therefore, the result of perspective insofar that we are socially constructed as our experiences are what mold us into who we are and what we deem to be important in terms of contribution and purpose. Anyway, that's enough of the history and sociology lesson, but I think this is helpful in explaining why we feel so lost and, for want of a better word, 'useless' if we don't have purpose in our lives. This, alongside the decrease in religion, may go some way to explain why we often struggle with our place in the world which impacts our well-being. And remember, having purpose is a key component of resilience during times of adversity. As Nietzsche said: *"He who has a why can endure any how"*.

When asked a lot of people will say their kids are their 'why' and yes, part of your 'why' may well be the people in your life, but it's so much bigger than that. Your purpose is your drive, your reason for living and getting out of the bed in the morning and, if you get it right, it will energise you and enhance your life in ways that I can't explain. What I can say though is that it'll make you feel bloody great. I have never felt happier than times where I've had purpose and goals in my life.

For some people finding purpose is easy, for others it's incredibly difficult. And our purposes are all different so it's really not something anyone else can help you with. Other people can guide you, but it's something you have to identify on your own, I'm afraid. However, there are ways to figure it out on your own; my favourite of which is the Japanese concept of ikigai.

At times in my life when I've been pretty low I've always found ikigai soothing and reassuring, as if it's telling me that things will get better and be alright if I can get my thoughts in order. A bit like resilience, ikigai has four pillars (and again if you do a quick internet search you'll find more pretty venn diagrams): passion; mission; vocation; and profession. These four are informed by four questions: what do you love (this is your passion and your mission); what does the world need from you (this is your mission and your vocation); what can you be paid to do (this is your vocation and your profession); and what are you good at (this is your profession and your passion). And, as with resilience, to reach your purpose or your 'reason for being' you need all four to overlap.

What I will also say is that to be truly satisfied with your purpose, it needs to align with your values so it is essential you understand what these are. This is why people who work in a job that is aligned to their values (that is, jobs that are more a vocation than simply a 'job') are happier and more content with their lives. Being able to make money from something you feel passionate about is a lovely feeling, because the chances are that this is your ikigai. Regardless of whether your purpose earns you money or not, you'll never be truly happy if it doesn't fit with your morals and values. So, you'll need to do a bit of work to discover what these are. What is it that you value in life? I've found it helpful to identify three or four values that are important to me, reflecting on these as I've refined my purpose. By doing this I've aligned my purpose with what I think is important in life which, in turn, will increase my life satisfaction and make me feel better.

At times when my mental health has been really poor I've thought a lot about my ikigai and I've spent many days pondering exactly what would bring me that complete and utter sense of purpose in my nihilist existence. It didn't just hit me, it took many years of trial and error and twists and turns because it's actually quite difficult to find something that gives you all four components of Ikigai *and* fits with your morals and values. And now, at 39-years-old, I think I've finally figured it out. Getting to this point wasn't easy and I've a lot of work ahead to actually achieve my purpose and bring me fulfilment and ikiagi.

Purpose comes in lots of forms and across many spheres of life. It might involve your kids. It might be your job (if you're one of those lucky people who've found their vocation). You might find purpose in contribution through volunteering or activism. Or maybe it's just something you simply enjoy doing. At this very moment, as I write, I feel motivated and full to the brim with energy (even though it's 2am and I have to be up for work early) because I feel a massive sense of purpose and contribution. If you don't know or are confused over your 'why' (and that's okay, because I don't think many of us ever give any real focused thought to what our 'purpose' is in life) a good place to start is figuring out your core values. Then, get out all manner of colourful pens, draw yourself a venn diagram of ikigai and get writing!

FINDING RESILIENCE

See how all the components of resilience are interlinked? We need to be self-aware to understand the impact of our actions on others and to enable us to develop positive supportive reciprocal relationships. We need to know when to look after ourselves through self-care and being mindful and by doing this we become more self-aware. Our self-awareness enables us to see the impact we have on others and helps us to identify and understand our 'why' to make our lives meaningful. All of this makes us happier, which makes us resilient which enables us to replenish our emotional 'reservoir'; our surge capacity. Which, of course, is why we've all been feeling so shitty this past year. So, there we are, resilience comes full circle.

And whilst all of this makes us more resilient, it also increases your capacity to help others who are going through a difficult time. You can't be a helpful support person if you've no resilience yourself. Well, you can, but only in the short-term and likely to the detriment of your own emotional well-being. So, put your mask on first then help others with theirs.

I know all of these things seem simple, but it's easy to forget when you're doing it tough. It's even easier to forget whilst feeling shit and in the midst of spinning all the plates of work, school, meetings, extra-curricular activities, social occasions, meal planning, holidays, housekeeping, sorting the finances, keeping on top of appointments and on and on it goes. Now, 2021 is actually a good time to think about what we can all do to improve our resilience because a lot of the external pressure has been removed. Use the 'quiet' (I use that term loosely as quiet is subjective and I know sure as hell my life isn't always 'quiet' right now!) time to look at where you can do some personal growth that will benefit your emotional well-being in the future. I've used the most recent lockdown to revisit my purpose, up my capacity for self-care, ditch my penchant for procrastination and start to take steps towards my goals. It feels productive. It feels good. And even though the start of 2021 brought probably one of the worst times of the whole COVID-19 escapade (and, in fact, of my life to date), I actually feel happier. I'm still sad about things that have happened that are out with my control, but I am happier and more content in myself. That's resilience (I still need to practice the mindfulness though).

There are many long-term benefits of resilience too. Being resilient doesn't have to be reactive; it can proactively improve your life too. The Bounce Back Project highlights all of these benefits as the outcome of being resilient: lower rate of mortality and improved physical health; reduced risk-taking behavior (e.g. negative coping strategies such as drugs and alcohol) and thus reduced risk of addiction; less absence from work/school; improved academic achievement and continued development; and greater involvement in community/family activities. Who'd not want that? So, you can start to see how being resilient can not only enable you to better recover from stress and trauma, but it can lead to better emotional, mental and physical health in the short- and the long-term. Win-win.

So, if you struggle with bouncing back from life's adversities and challenges (or even those enormous shitty road blocks that life sometimes seems to lay down one after the other), work on developing these five aspects of your life. Now, life isn't always good, there will be bad parts and awful things to deal with – I know I've had my fair share, and I'm also aware that I'm luckier than some who've had it significantly worse than me. Adversity and challenge are part of life. You will face heartache, relationship breakdowns, death, illness, accidents, loneliness, financial stress and other trauma – I'm afraid that's life. The trick is how we avoid that downward spiral that threatens to overwhelm us when we face significant stress in life. If you don't want to languish, if you want to flourish (or, dare I say it, have all of Maslow's hierarchy of needs fulfilled and reach ultimate life satisfaction!), then you need to find a way to deal with adversity and life stress, or find a way for it to motivate you.

I have a colleague who is one of the most positive, inspiring and motivated people you could ever meet. Recently I had the pleasure of chatting about her life and career and it absolutely blew me away. I came out of the (virtual) meeting really quite emotional having heard her journey. I won't go into detail as it's not my story to tell but the struggles she has faced in her life – through absolutely no fault of her own – are phenomenal. Yet, every time she was faced with significant stress, she grasped it as an opportunity to learn. And she has; she has achieved so much through channeling her energy into positivity and productivity. She has shown incredible resilience and, despite the adversity she has faced in her life and no matter how bad it got, she flourished.

This isn't to say that you won't sometimes feel as if your life is on a downward spiral, unfortunately you probably will. Sorry folks. But, if you strengthen your power of resilience through the five pillars then bouncing back will become a hell of a lot easier. Do the work now and you'll thank yourself the next time you come up against even the biggest and shittiest of life stress.

LESSONS IN POSITIVITY

"Do not let the behaviour of others destroy your inner peace" (Dalai Lama)

It's no secret that 2020/2021 was a time like no other; a time where the proverbial shit hit the fan. It was like living in a giant washing machine – we were tossed around, spun, spat out and wrung out to dry. There is a lot to be said for blissful ignorance, or burying your head in the sand, particularly when it comes to a worldwide pandemic, political turmoil and conflict. Toxicity and negativity were rife in the world, there was conflict at every turn and it was all played out all day, every day through the curse of 24/7 news channels and social media. I've already explained the concept of surge capacity and the impact this has on our ability to cope, our resilience and our well-being. But, when we think about self-care we often overlook the importance of limiting negativity and reducing toxicity in your life.

SAY GOODBYE TO TOXICITY

The severing – or, in cases where this is not possible (such as a family member or work colleague), severely curtailing – of personal relationships that are detrimental to your well-being can be very difficult and requires emotional strength. But you first need to acknowledge and accept that the relationship is toxic; that it is not good for you.

So, what is a toxic relationship and how do you recognise one? Simply put if a relationship leaves you feeling unhappy, drained, disappointed and unsupported then there's a good chance it's toxic, regardless of whether it's a partner, family member, friend or acquaintance. Relationship experts all stress the importance of limiting toxic relationships, ideally ending them where possible, for your well-being. Recognising this type of relationship is easy from the outside, but when you're part of that relationship, it can often be hard to identify, particularly where that person is a partner, close family member or close friend. My advice though, is listen to people if they tell you that there's something not quite right about a relationship in your life – often they're looking at it objectively and can see the warning signs. There are many symptoms and signs of a toxic relationship, including: feeling on edge; lack of support; jealousy; controlling behaviour; overt or passive aggression; lack of empathy; resentment; ignoring your needs (particularly during difficult life events); disrespect; and accusations/blame. There are many, many more. Now, these things often rear their head in a healthy relationship too and that's normal. But, if it happens frequently, you're always the one apologising and/or you find yourself avoiding that person then there's a good chance that the relationship is toxic and the other party is, what I like to call, an emotional vampire (this doesn't make them bad, it just makes them bad for your emotional well-being).

Severing or curtailing a relationship with someone who has been a part of your life or whom you have a strong emotional connection with is incredibly difficult and painful – I know, I've been there a few times. But, if you feel that the relationship is toxic than I'd bet that the other party also feels that way. It's exhausting trying to maintain a relationship with someone who is not good for you. This doesn't mean either of you are bad people, just that you're not good people for each other. It takes a lot of strength to admit when a relationship has run its course and become a negative influence on your life.

Severing a toxic relationship can be easier than curtailing one. It is more straightforward as you no longer need to see the other person again. Although this is difficult, it can be easier than curtailing a relationship with someone whom you will have to see or communicate with regularly, such as a family member or a work colleague. It's simply not practical nor always possible to cut a family member or work colleague out of your life – there will always be family gatherings (unless you're in the midst of a worldwide pandemic, of course!) and you can't just stop talking to someone you work with (although wouldn't that be nice?). Managing and navigating these relationships can be very tricky and requires a strong will and firm boundaries, such as limiting contact as much as possible, making it clear what you can and cannot help them with and avoiding issues that you know will provoke conflict (you know, like politics and religion!).

When it comes to ending a relationship with someone whom increases negativity in your life it can prove useful to speak to trusted friends and family (obviously those with whom you have a mutually supportive positive relationship). In my experience when toxic relationships have come to an end, those friends and family I confided in afterwards have been very supportive, provided reassurance and, in most cases, expressed surprise that it hadn't happened sooner (I told you it's much easier to see toxicity looking from the outside in). Like I said, it's easier to completely cut ties but this does not mean it's easy. It's very upsetting to end a relationship that's run its course and has turned toxic, regardless of the reason or how it made you feel. That person was likely there for you at some point in your life and going your separate ways is fairly gut wrenching.

I'm a strong believer in relationships being there for different stages in your life – and this is especially true for friendships. For example, one of my best friends I've known for nearly 20 years. We were great friends for a good few years but then we lost touch because our lives just went in different directions and this caused a bit of conflict. However, our friendship was rekindled years later and now we're probably closer than we've ever been. Why? Our lives dovetailed back together and oddly enough we just forgot about the conflict that drove us apart because it was no longer important. This isn't always the case, and I have also had some toxic relationships that ended pretty acrimoniously with people whom I no longer have anything to do with. It's not pleasant and can be very distressing, yet it's important to acknowledge that that relationship wasn't good for you in the first place. The pain you feel when a toxic relationship ends is real, but it will fade and, in the end, you will feel lighter and better for it.

I can't tell you how to end a toxic relationship, there's plenty of advice on that online and from relationship experts, but I can personally vouch for how much better you will feel without this negativity in your life. Life is difficult enough, particularly life during 2020/2021, without choosing to maintain an unhealthy relationship or let it unduly sap the happiness from you. Put simply, why flog a dead horse? Cut your losses, wish each other peace and happiness and move on. Life is too short.

WE ARE WHAT WE CONSUME

You've heard the saying 'you are what you eat'? Well, you are also what you consume. Humans are sociable beings and we need interaction and connection. During lockdown this has been hindered significantly and our connection has come through the virtual world. It makes sense then that our mindset becomes a reflection of what we consume virtually and, in 2020/21, that is predominantly through the news and social media.

News media

The news has an incredible impact on our lives and it is nigh on impossible to escape it. We have newspapers (albeit now a dying breed), 24/7 rolling news coverage, online news, books, magazines, TV programmes and social media (which I'll speak about separately, although for the purposes of news I will refer to the social media channels of news organisations, such as the BBC). It takes one hell of a conscious effort to avoid the news – those of you who've ever tried to avoid finding out a football score or what happened in the last episode of a popular series before you've had time to watch it yourself will be aware of quite how difficult it can be! Yet whilst staying informed about the going's on in the world is important, the impact of 24/7 access to the news can actually have a detrimental impact on your well-being. In today's world we simply cannot escape the news unless we make a very concerted effort.

Take, for example, the news coverage of the 2001 9/11 terrorist attacks in the US or the 7/7 2005 bombings across London. It was constant. It was on every news channel, on every radio station and emblazoned across every newspaper for weeks upon weeks. Pictures of those poor souls in the World Trade Centre as they fell; photos of the mangled bus in Tavistock Square in London; photos of those missing. It was everywhere. Then there's the impact of the rolling news coverage of the 2001 War on Terror and 2003 Iraq War. These wars were unprecedented in that they were the first wars to have 24/7 news coverage; day or night we could switch on a news channel and see images from the front line of bombings, gun fire and all the damage that that causes. Now, much of the research quite rightly focuses on the mental health impact of war on military personnel or on Afghani and Iraqi civilians, but I remember watching the news coverage in my early 20's and being deeply affected by it. I remember watching that first bomb drop on 19th March 2003 in 'Operation Iraqi Freedom' and watching the news the next day as missile after missile landed in Baghdad. I remember the feeling of utter sadness and helplessness as all I could think about were the innocent civilians. I also knew (and thankfully still do) a number of UK Army and RAF personnel who I knew would be in the very first phases of that invasion and, try as I might, it was difficult not to think of them amongst it all. Whilst COVID-19 is different to war, the stories in this book highlight that I'm not alone in the distress that too much news consumption can cause.

There are thousands upon thousands of articles on the impact of the media on mental health and well-being, most focusing on the stress-inducing nature of the news. In general, news tends to focus on negatives: environmental disasters; wars; death; crime; catastrophic accidents; political divisiveness; and so on. Yes, there is the odd 'good news story', but they are few and far between and normally reserved for local newspapers and/or regional TV news. It's probably of no surprise to you that the news can bring you stress and stress, as we know, is linked to depression, anxiety and addiction. An article *'Dealing with Anxiety and Stress in the Age of the 24/7 News Cycle'* that was published in March 2020 (before the impact of COVID-19 was really acknowledged by the UK and the US) explained:

> *"Whether it's the coronavirus (COVID-19), political divisiveness, threats of terrorism, or mass shootings in*

malls, churches, and schools, it seems like there is always something to worry about. You might not be immediately affected by these issues, but the constant exposure to 24-hour news and social media, which is often heavily skewed toward the negative, can adversely influence your mental health and overall well-being…If you're finding yourself becoming more and more anxious in the face of a constant barrage of bad news, you're not alone."

Unlike previous world events, there is no escaping the news as it is in your home and all around you all the time. It is at a touch of a fingertip at any hour of any day; and that is not healthy. I think it was back in 2017/18 that I heard the term 'headline stress disorder' and it's so true – the impact of news headlines and coverage is without a doubt damaging our mental health and well-being. News coverage of the pandemic is no different and the findings of research *'COVID-19 and the 24/7 News Cycle: Does COVID-19 News Exposure Affect Mental Health?'* conducted in the US in March 2020 (reported in 'Socius: Sociological Research for a Dynamic World') explains:

"The coronavirus disease 2019 (COVID-19) pandemic has upended nearly every aspect of social life in the United States and abroad. People turn to news to provide public health updates about the virus, such as reports of new cases and deaths, but also to understand how COVID-19 is affecting jobs and the economy. The news, irrespective of its format, serves as a central conduit of information during the pandemic. Prior research examining public traumas, such as terrorist attacks, suggests that greater media intake may also amplify perceived threats about the virus and therefore

Now, after reading that, tell me that being able to waken up and the first thing you do is reaching for your phone to check the news is in any way good for your mental health? No, I didn't think so. Not long into the pandemic I made a very conscious effort to stop watching the news. In some ways I was lucky as I have a colleague who is very knowledgeable about public health so I knew I could always ask her about certain COVID-related developments and she would give me factual and balanced information. But I know not everyone's as lucky as I am to have that. I stopped watching Ministerial and Government briefings (apart from the Janey Godley voiceovers, but more on that later), I stopped reading news articles and I actively avoided any news about COVID-19. I wasn't being ignorant to it, I just didn't want it to consume every minute of every hour or my waking day. I have to say, it was refreshing to be free of the shackles of it. And the stories in this book tell me I'm not the only one that felt that way. So, switch off the news, delete the news apps from your phone and breathe a sigh of relief!

The mental health impact of news coverage isn't just about the volume of news you consume, it's about the type and quality of news you consume. When I embarked on the final year of my undergraduate degree in 2003 it came time to choose a topic for my undergraduate dissertation. I'd done all manner of courses as part of my Bachelor degree but the one I found utterly fascinating was about crimes of the powerful which included the role that the mass media plays in the accountability and scrutinisation of those in power. Anyway, I'm not here to talk about my studies but in the process of reading the literature on the topic I developed a heightened awareness of the sheer power of the news media which I have never shaken, in particular a deep distrust of the 24/7 rolling news that surrounds us (and has, in fact, grown in the prevailing 18 years). And this is before we even start to think about the very real, very present use of censorship and media propaganda (no this isn't limited to media coverage of World Wars I and II, there is evidence of governments paying for 'fake' news for propaganda even to this day).

What my studies all those years ago left me with is a very healthy dose of scepticism over all media content; from the stuff I agreed with to the stuff I didn't, from print to online to TV news coverage, all of it is skewed in one way or another. Media companies are very powerful beasts, one look at Rupert Murdoch's right-wing conservative media empire shows the impact of the media on politics and public opinion. Unfortunately, it's impossible to escape media bias and it exists as much on the left (liberalism) as it does on the right (conservativism). I challenge anyone to find news that isn't even a little biased; even those who think they're being objective will have inadvertently allowed their own unconscious biases to impact on their writing (even independent journalists have selected to cover a story for a reason). It's becoming increasingly difficult to find news sources that are completely honest and accurate. This wouldn't necessarily be a problem if everyone was news media literate and understood the politicisation of the media but this is not the case.

Many people take what they hear, see and read in the news as gospel; they don't question it nor do they look for alternative opinions. During the COVID-19 pandemic this became incredibly worrying at best, dangerous at worst, as mistruths and conspiracy theories were perpetuated by the media. Interestingly, The Poynter Institute (a non-profit in Florida, US) has been conducting research and training and producing resources focussing on improving news media literacy. But this will only work if everyone adopts the same approach to better understanding the politics of the media and has a healthy dose of scepticism for the things they read, hear and see.

Now, I don't know about you, but seeing coverage of things that I think are complete and utter shit really pisses me off. There are many examples of this, but I'll stick to examples in relation to the pandemic and lockdown to illustrate my point: the Dominic Cummings/Barnard Castle fiasco, the President Trump/bleach injecting absurdity, the politicisation of the Scotland/England border closure and different approaches to vaccination programmes...once again, I could go on. As watching/reading/listening to these start to get me frustrated and angry, I feel my heart beat a little faster and my blood pressure go up. I have to make a conscious and concerted effort to avoid the media for a bit. I know my opinions on things and if I believe that news coverage is irresponsible, inaccurate and/or gets me riled up then it's time to switch off and watch that trashy movie or read that trashy book. There are a lot more important things for me to focus on; and my well-being is at the very top of that list! So, if it annoys you or you don't agree with it then turn it off. You don't need that stress in your life; not on top of everything else. You'll feel much better for it.

I'm not at all surprised at the stories from people in this book who had to switch off the news and stop reading the coverage of the COVID-19 pandemic as I've found myself doing this for years – the 9/11, 2001 War on Terror, 2003 Iraq War, 7/7, the 2007/08 global financial crisis and stock market crash, the 2014 Scottish independence referendum, the 2016 Brexit referendum, the 2016 US Presidential election, the 2020 Presidential election and even some of the more pleasant news stories, such as Royal and celebrity babies and weddings (babies and weddings are always nice, but there's a limit to the longevity of such 'news'). You get the gist.

Sometimes, staying away from the news is better for you. It doesn't mean you have to be ignorant to what's going on, but you certainly don't need to be bombarded with it. It's completely up to you how you cultivate the news you consume, don't be a passive consumer and make informed media literate choices based on what's best for you and your well-being. Just because the news is available 24/7 doesn't mean we should consume it 24/7. If it upsets you, worries you, angers you or starts to make you feel complacently numb then it's time to take a step back. You'll feel calmer, less anxious and significantly more in control.

Social media

As with the importance of limiting your news intake, there is something to be said for managing the social media content you see on a daily basis. This may seem a simple concept, but often people struggle. Social media can be a great thing – it connects us when we can't physically connect, it can enlighten us and teach us and make us laugh and cry. But it can also damage us. I'm not going to get into the big social media debate about whether it is good or bad, but I want to impart some advice specifically in relation to how you can use it to make yourself feel better. But, it's a bit like limiting the impact of the toxic people in your life – it can be quite difficult.

The first bit is easy: read things that make you happy. Early on in lockdown I made a conscious effort to follow only inspiring and uplifting social media accounts. I didn't want to be deluged with negativity every time I opened my Facebook or Instagram. Jeez, I was getting enough of that from the news. I followed things that promoted positivity, made me laugh or distracted me from the daily infection rate, political saga or family drama. I shared cute videos of giant pandas playing in the snow, silly videos of cats and dogs, funny (and a little rude) voice-over videos from Janey Godley (if you haven't seen them you really need to check them out!). Little things like this really cheered me up and I figured if they made me laugh then they'd maybe make others laugh too. I WhatsApped and Facebook Messengered friends and family with silly videos or funny memes or ridiculous stories.

Now, the second bit…well, that's harder. I have friends and family who really struggle with this and, as with dealing with toxic people in life, you have to be quite brutal. The basic premise is that you cultivate your social media to show only the things that uplift you that I've discussed above. The other side of this is that you need to limit the negativity you ingest via social media or your messages. Parts of this are fairly straightforward: unfollow random pages that post things you don't agree with or make you sad, angry or shocked; leave group chats that sap your energy or cultivate negative thoughts or feelings; and unfollow 'celebrities' or 'influencers' (or whatever other name you want to call them) if what they post makes you angry or feel bad about yourself or your life. Who needs to see things from someone you don't know or don't like who has beliefs and opinions completely at odds with yours? Following accounts/people who make you feel bad – for whatever reason – do not help you. Unfollow and delete!

So, what about the random things that pop up on your social media? Or the comments on something you posted that piss you off so much you can feel your heart race? You can't not see them once you've seen them, that is true. But it falls back to old adage: *'you can only control your actions'*. My advice to you is simple – scroll on by! You don't need to engage. You have the power to not let it bother you, no matter how much you disagree with it. Water off a ducks back and all that!

I've already spoken about the importance of limiting what you watch on the news. As great as rolling news can be, it has meant that we can't escape from the horrors going on across the world – wars, disasters, violence…and the pandemic.   But you can remove yourself from it by not watching it. I want to talk about doing that with social media. What I've noticed during this time is that some platforms are worse than others at making you feel bad. Now, I use Facebook and Instagram and I'll occasionally have a look at Twitter, although I don't have an account. Of all the inspiring people I follow there seems to be a commonality – Twitter brings out the worst in people (and Facebook too, to a lesser extent). I lost count of the number of people I follow on Facebook or Instagram who were abused and/or trolled on Twitter. Why? Honestly, I don't have a clue. A lot of investigation has been done on why this is and there seems to be a widely accepted agreement that Twitter is more toxic than other social media platforms, and a lot of explanation and speculation as to why. From what I can gather the main reason for the toxicity, abuse, hate and harassment stems from Twitter's lack of oversight. I don't know enough about it to comment and regardless my message isn't about Twitter *per se* anyway, because the same can be said for any one of the social media platforms today, so really my message is this: if one of the platforms (or even all of them) can change your mood and you find yourself unable to control this or your reaction to what you see then I have some simple advice – delete! If you find social media bad for your well-being then delete your profile, or at least delete it from your phone and log out of it on your laptop. If it makes you feel bad then the less interaction you have with it, the better. So, delete it, or limit it. You will feel all the better for it. One of my absolute favourite and inspiring people to follow, Matt Haig (you absolutely must read his books – fiction and non-fiction to give your mental health a wee boost), summed it up perfectly on one of his social media posts:

> *"Feel so much better after leaving [platform]. I hadn't realised how much the negativity and snark was getting to me. How grumpy it made me. I am a better person without it. I think [platform] is fine for some people. But I was too sensitive for it. I couldn't cope with it and I truly believe it was, like a drug, changing my moods and behaviour a little bit. I was getting cross about things in a disproportionate way. I was out of tune with myself on there and plugged into a kind of outrage machine. A place where too often people find it easier to be good in the abstract but mean in their conduct to fellow humans."*

And lastly, what of the family and friends who post things on social media that make you feel bad? This is the hard part and I admit to struggling with this myself in the past. Take my mum, for example. I love her to bits and we have the same moral and ethical values and broadly similar ideological and political beliefs but we have been known to argue to the point of tears over certain things. In every referendum and every election, her and I have cast our votes the same way (we discuss this stuff in our family, you see). Yet during both the Scottish Independence and Brexit referendums I could feel myself becoming more and more agitated with her continual social media posts. Now, I mostly agreed with them yet her social media was overpowering, as if I was being barraged (I use this term to describe the feeling of being constantly clobbered over the head). I'm quite politically engaged and I enjoy healthy political debate, but my goodness, I was sick of seeing her twenty-gazillion posts a day. But what to do? I considered unfriending her – yep, unfriending my own mum – on Facebook but, I thought, I can't do that, she's my mum!! It was easier with acquaintances who shared things I could feel making my blood boil – unfriending them was easy. But my mum? I could unfollow her, but then I would miss the nice bits she posted – the family photos, the funny memes and videos. Yes, I could scroll past her political posts as I did with those that popped up randomly on my newsfeed, but believe me when I tell you the amount of posts she shared would've made that extremely difficult (I wonder actually how she got anything done in those days if I'm honest...). In the end I opted to unfollow her. I didn't tell her, well, not at the time anyway, but I have since and we both had a bit of a giggle about it and now she knows that I will probably do the same if/when it happens again. The simple message here is that if your social media feed makes you feel anything negative – anything at all, even if it's just as simple as information overload – then you need to do something about it.

Social media really does impact on people in a real visceral way. I know people who just can't move past some of the comments that have been directed at them. Can't not reply to something that annoys them (I can be bad for this myself). Are unable to look at pictures and understand that it isn't a reflection of that person's whole life. Constantly assume that a meme or a quote posted is directed at them. But, social media isn't inherently bad. It's a social construction. It's how we use it that makes it bad. By changing my attitude and how I interact with social media I change the discourse of what I see every day. It is within your ability to cultivate what you see every day and control your reaction to it. It's true what Matt Haig said, if you read anger you'll feel anger. So, get rid of the negativity and you'll never look back.

Find inspiring content

But consumption doesn't start and end with the news and social media. It's pretty much everywhere you look. There's books you read, podcasts you listen to, films and documentaries you watch...your mood can be altered by any one of these things and more. What I found myself doing during the pandemic and lockdown (as I have during other difficult periods in my life) is seeking out positive influence to consume. Podcasts are great for that and there's so many out there to meet your own needs and interests and they really can pick you up from a slump.

Television and movie-wise I'm a sucker for escapism –a smiley happy love story, a period drama, a war movie, a political drama or a complete escape from reality in a dystopian apocalypse (okay, so the last two might not quite be an escape from our current COVID-19 2020/21 political reality, but they normally do the trick!). But, sometimes I find myself feeling a little depressed if I watch too much of this kind of content; finding myself thinking that my life is utterly devoid of anything interesting. It's total crap, of course, and logically I know that. My life is as interesting as the next person's. But feelings aren't logic.

So, what do I do when I feel like this? Well, as with podcasts, I seek out inspirational things to watch – movies, documentaries, series, biopics. Again, there are plenty out there depending upon what you find uplifting. I love to watch those travel programmes about people living off the grid, or people who've sold up to move to some remote part of the world and live a simpler life, or people who've decided to convert the tiniest of little spaces into their home. I hate, with a vengeance, reality TV and I watch hardly any (although I did find myself watching *'Love at First Sight'* and *'Below Deck'* – what a pile of crap but jeez are they addictive!). The reality TV I do watch tends to involve cooking or tidying (I do like a bit of *'MasterChef'* and Marie Kondo). God, I sound boring. I'm not. Well, not all the time.

Basically, when I need to lift my mood I watch things that inspire me and encourage me to be more optimistic about the potential of my own life. It's amazing the power that this can have over your thoughts. If you're struggling for inspiration there are a few of my fail safe's that never cease to make me feel better: *'Minimalism: A Documentary About the Important Things'*; *'Heal'*; *'Becoming'; 'Resilience: The Biology of Stress and the Science of Hope'; 'Happy';* and *'Embrace: The Documentary'*. I come away from these smiling and feeling hopeful. Honestly, try them. Alternatively, something utterly ludicrous gets my vote – whether this be a hilarious comedy (you know, the kind that makes you belly chuckle till your sides hurt) or a mockumentary (so far, my favourite has to be *'Death to 2020'* on Netflix and yes, I know it was slated by the 'critics' but my dry Scots humour had me chuckling away!).

THE COMPARISON QUAGMIRE

What became abundantly clear to me as I compiled these amazing stories – is that we should never judge or compare our lives to those of others. Now, in normal circumstances I know this and I'm sure most people do and are able to exercise restraint in that respect. But, for some reason, lockdown and the pandemic did a complete one-eighty shift on my perceptions of others. As I sat in my wee flat staring at the same walls, desperately trying to block out the noise of the Xbox/YouTube and the kids trying to kill each other, trying not to see the utter bùrach (that's Scots Gaelic for a right mess) that my flat was turning into, watching mindless TV and – depending on the time of day – drinking either a coffee or large glass of pinot grigio (sometimes I felt fancy and went for the prosecco) I found myself drowning in the depths of social media and others' organised, productive and happy looking lives.

It'll come as no surprise that some of the stories in this book are from people I know – some well, some not so well – as well as complete strangers. But it may come as a surprise that some of these people are those whom I saw on their social media as coping wonderfully with lockdown and all that it entailed. It wasn't until I got their stories for this book and they laid their souls bare in their words that it hit me how wrong I'd been – that those people that I'd been admiring had been suffering too and that their productivity or routine was their coping mechanism for their own struggles. I know you must be thinking: but you know some of these people, surely you knew that was their coping mechanism? You'd think, wouldn't you? But I genuinely didn't. I looked at their Facebook, Twitter and Instagram and thought they were achieving so much so they must've been loving it. How wrong I was!

So, my last word of wisdom and the moral of this story, is do not judge your own life from what you see on other people's social media. Deep down we all know that this projection is the 'highlight reel' of people's lives, I'm guilty of that same thing as I post a picture of the kids sitting nicely eating their 'ramen' (aka instant noodles - in all honesty, I do actually make ramen on occasion – just not today!). Why would you post loads of negative things and lay your soul bare for all 279 people to see (some of whom you've spent only one hour with once in a hotel bar on holiday)? We don't want to seem as if our lives have gone tits up and we certainly don't want to be seen as needy. So, remember that – remember that our stoicism is what produces the content on our social media and that outwardly wonderful life we all lead is a fallacy. It simply doesn't exist all the time. Sure, we have good times, but we have bad times too. That's part of life and it can't be good all the time. We need to stop punishing ourselves for being human.

You will not, as the zillions of life coaches or Insta influencers out there are constantly indoctrinating their followers to believe on an hourly basis, 'live your best life' all the time. Hell, you probably won't even live it most of the time. But you will live it some of the time. Stop punishing yourself for something that is completely and utterly unattainable, particularly during times of trauma and uncertainty. Life isn't meant to be all love sunshine and roses, unfortunately. The bad comes with the good. But it makes the good all that much better.

And it's true what they say, even when it doesn't feel like it: we grow and learn way more from our failures and challenges than we do from success. Remember that. I promise, it helps.

THE VALUE OF CONTRIBUTION & KINDNESS

I have always been motivated by making a difference – in my personal and professional life. At work I am not motivated by status or money, but instead by the belief that the work I do makes a difference to people's lives. That's where I get satisfaction, not from promotion or 'climbing the ladder'. My desire to give something back and improve the world – no matter how small – doesn't end outside of my paid work. I do a number of voluntary roles that all revolve around making things better, ensuring people are treated fairly and that their well-being is considered at all times. Why? Well, I've always been driven by social justice but I remember watching *'Minimalism: A Documentary About the Important Things'* and then reading the book *'Minimalism: Live a Meaningful Life'* and being inspired by the focus it placed on the importance of contribution. The authors both experienced life-changing events that made them question their lives and they both came to realise that the five most important things in life were: health, relationships, passion, growth and contribution. For me, this links back to the importance of 'purpose' in our ability to demonstrate resilience in the face of adversity and the quest for Ikigai – that ultimate reason for us to get out of bed every day. As with resilience, you need all five things to be truly happy and so contribution becomes an inextricable part of your happiness.

Numerous studies have linked kindness with good mental health and subjective well-being; there's a great guide *'Kindness Matters'* from the Mental Health Foundation that goes into the relationship between kindness and mental health in more detail. In fact, kindness is so important to both our own and collective public mental health and well-being, that it was the theme of Mental Health Awareness Week 2020 in the UK in light of the impact of COVID-19.

I'm not going to get into the science of it again, as we've spoken about it already, but acts of kindness actually increases dopamine, oxytocin and serotonin production, all of those lovely 'happy hormones' that make us feel better. Kindness towards others also facilitates kindness towards ourselves and enables us to better understand our own emotions, experiences and responses (that is, it helps us to become more self-aware) and more mindful in that we appreciate the here and the now. Being kind also improves our relationships, support networks and strengthens our connections all the while making us happier; in fact, a study by the Harvard Business School found that countries whose people were more charitable and financially generous were the happiest societies. Furthermore, kindness is the ticket to increased humanity and humility which will enable us to target worldwide inequality as we strive for more meaningful and happier lives.

There's a reason ikigai aligns with our 'reason for getting out of bed' and our innate sense of fulfilment, purpose and authenticity. Furthermore, we already know about the importance of purpose and contribution in enhancing our resilience. So, by practicing kindness to others you'll learn to be kind to yourself and give your mental health and resilience a much-needed boost. What's not to love?

A number of the memoirs in the *'Life in Lockdown Duology'* include discussions of volunteering during the pandemic and lockdown: delivering prescriptions; helping at food banks; delivering food; and/or checking in on vulnerable neighbours. All of these people volunteered during COVID-19 to make a difference and to introduce some positivity during a stressful and uncertain time and all reaped rewards in doing so. Their volunteering didn't just make life better for those they were helping, but also for themselves as it channeled their energy, gave them purpose and made them feel good about themselves as they were doing something to help others.

Contribution doesn't have to come by way of volunteering and, whilst it undoubtedly brings satisfaction, it isn't without its challenges. Take, for example, the childminder who took in vulnerable children during the pandemic to the detriment of her own family and the shop manager who refused to put his staff in harm's way and offered his resignation to stand up for what he thought was right. Both of these stories show the extreme side of the personal sacrifice of contribution, yet neither regretted their actions or decisions, despite the challenges. These were simply acts of kindness, albeit in the context of their employment. But kindness is kindness and sacrifice is sacrifice. I like to think of these examples as moral kindness; the standing up for or doing what's right, regardless of personal sacrifice.

A lot of people talk about kindness in a fairly abstract way, but there are plenty of easy ways to show kindness to others. I love nothing more than a random act of kindness: paying for someone's coffee without them knowing; leaving a book lying somewhere for someone else to find; letting someone cut in front of me in the supermarket queue; paying for someone's shopping if they don't have enough money; donating a prize win to someone in more need; and so on. I do it a lot and it feels good. I don't do it for myself, I do it for others but I can't deny the mood boost it brings. The key here is to not expect anything in return, except perhaps for the recipient of your kindness to pass it on. The theory is that random acts of kindness will snowball and the world will become a nicer, kinder and more pleasant place. And it works. In a virtual work team meeting during lockdown, a colleague told us that in the days that followed McDonald's re-opening that the car in front of her had paid for their order; she said it made her day and completely lifted her spirits. Of course, she paid for the order behind her and hopefully on and on it went as people's days were made and their spirits lifted. They're not big nor (hopefully) expensive acts of kindness, but they can go a long way to putting a smile on someone's face.

There are other acts of kindness too, the wee things we do for the people we love and care about. I love to send cards and letters to people for no other reason than to make them smile; this is something I've done for years and has become more important since the pandemic restricted our social contact. Not long into lockdown I sent my mum, dad and gran a heap of photographs that would make them smile along with a wee note. My mum has sent my kids wee parcels of sweeties, glow in the dark pebbles, cards and the odd paper note (much to their delight!). I've sent my friends pamper packs and books. I've sent friends who're having a tough time self-care packages with cards and wee gestures of support. Consequently – and never asked for – I have received these gestures in return. I can't tell you how nice it is to get a random wee parcel on the doorstep amidst the bills and all the other crap. I've had cards and photographs in the post, flowers left on the doorstep and some beautiful flowers delivered for both happy and sad occasions. Just the other day, in fact, I got a 'pocket hug' with a card from a friend – for no other reason than 'just because'. It doesn't just stop at the post either as some people are not able to do this for varying reasons and I have friends who send me the funniest and loveliest messages and memes for no reason, they just pop up at random times and make me laugh or smile, wee sayings like: *'one of the weirdest things about being an adult is having a favourite hob ring, yet nobody talks about it'*, *'one day you will tell your story of how you've overcome what you're going through now, and it will become part of someone else's survival guide'*, *'in a zombie apocalypse I'd eat you last'* and *'if you were stung by a jellyfish I'd totally pee on you'*. I think my favourite of the lockdown era has to be the comparison of fetal ultrasound pictures to Edvard Munich's 'Scream' (honestly, Google it, it's pretty freaky!). These are all pretty inconsequential and silly little gestures but by goodness they have the power to make you smile (if not erupt into that ridiculous belly laughter we've all forgotten as we've got older and more boring).

If life is stressing you out and you're feeling low, find a way to contribute – look for causes to support or ways to volunteer your time to make life more bearable for others. I know that I'm at my happiest when I feel as if I'm contributing something or making life better for someone, no matter how big or small, whether it be through work, volunteering, random acts of kindness or even my writing. So, send that card or silly meme, for nothing more than to brighten up someone else's day or, even better, do something for a stranger with the expectation of absolutely nothing in return. Think of a way you can contribute to the world and make it happen (this book is an example, alongside many other books). Have a look for opportunities to volunteer your time, a cause to support or any other way you can help (donating unwanted goods to a homeless shelter or women's refuge, for example). It doesn't have to be big grand gestures to make a difference to someone's life.

Giving back is simply about kindness and tends to involve an element of personal sacrifice (except the memes, they're free!); whether it's through your time, resources or impact. However, the social return on investment is phenomenal and I can't emphasise enough how much giving back (in whatever way) enriches your life and improves your well-being. It doesn't cost to be kind (unless you want it to), yet the power of kindness is phenomenal – it really does make the world a better place to be.

PERSPECTIVE: THE POWER OF POSITIVE THINKING

'Life in Lockdown II' discusses the potential positives of COVID-19 on a much larger scale, but it's pertinent to all of us

individually too. What struck me about the stories in this book was the evolution of each individuals' journey through the pandemic and lockdown. I knew I'd definitely learnt from my 2020 lockdown experience and implemented change in my life to make 2021 infinitely more bearable. It wasn't easy and it required change and motivation in spades. But recall some of the stories you've just read and you'll see the importance of change and reframing your thoughts and feelings in improving your life. Sure, it's unlikely it will result in an immediate material change to your actual circumstances but it will help you realise that some things are out of your control and help you to identify potential solutions and be open to new ideas that you might not otherwise have considered.

I will take my experiences, thoughts and feelings from this strange period in time and learn from it. I will look after myself better, whatever that may mean. I will not settle for mediocre. I will not tolerate toxicity. Gone is giving presents instead of my presence. Writing this has made me think back to a year of 'presence' giving in 2017 where, instead of a gift I took my loved ones to do something they enjoyed and we did it together. It was some year and took me out of my comfort zone: sphering (you ever tried rolling down a hill inside a giant inflatable ball?); stand-up jet-skiing on Loch Lomond; the London Concertante play Vivaldi; horse-riding; cream tea cruise up the Forth; snowboarding on Glen Nevis (where I broke my wrist – oops!); ballet; scuba diving lessons; and, of course, the obligatory afternoon teas and spa days (hey, it's not my fault my friends like a pamper too!). In return my friends did the same (I didn't ask them to, but the practice kind of rubbed off on them) and I was treated to more ballet, afternoon teas, spa days, helicopter rides and many other new and wonderful things. And the best thing about it – I spent time with the people I care about in ways I wouldn't normally. Thinking about it now, I don't know why I stopped doing that – it was way more special than a material gift, I don't want to sound all hippy-dippy but it was the gift of time (and fun, lots of fun)!

So, whilst I can't control how our wider society learns from our collective experience, I know for certain that my life will look and feel different. This book is an example of that. No more sitting thinking about things I'd like to do; it's time to *do* them. You hear a lot of people going on about the Law of Attraction and it's true, it works. But it isn't simply sitting 'manifesting' (I don't like that word as it implies passiveness) something into existence. It's about bringing your desires into reality through your thoughts, emotions, beliefs and, crucially, your actions.

There are a number of examples of this in the pages of this book. The power of positive thinking is phenomenal (people often refer to this as 'practicing gratitude' but that's a term I don't particularly like and, in fear of being shot down, it has connotations that we're not grateful – so I much prefer the term positive thinking). What the stories in the *'Life in Lockdown Duology'* have in common is that each person recognised if they were struggling, reframed their thinking to focus on the positives of the situation they were in and implemented change to make things better. That, my friend, is all that the Law of Attraction and 'manifesting' really is, and it's within every single person's gift. It all starts with positive thinking and a little perspective.

It's hard sometimes and we all fall foul to wallowing, even those who are emotionally healthy and have resilience in abundance. It's okay to feel bad sometimes – it's part of life and being human – but using positive thinking, putting things into perspective and taking action will help to shorten your stay in that dark corner of your mind. I'm as guilty as the next person for falling into that trap.

The other day when I was moaning about lockdown, my son turned to me and said: *'Well, it's not as bad as Anne Frank though is it, mum?'* Put in my place by a nine-year-old. Out of the mouths of babes, indeed.

A PERSONAL REFLECTION ON COPING, RESILIENCE & POSTIVITY – IT'S TIME TO THRIVE

As I write this final chapter, it's just been announced that Scotland's lockdown is to start easing, with the hope that by June 2021 we can return to some kind of normality. Vaccines are being rolled out across the country – and indeed the world – and we all patiently wait our turn in the hope that this will be what we need to be able to emerge into the world again, hug our loved ones and make up for the year we've lived in purgatory. It's been a strange old year. Not great, but not awful either. It's been good, but also bad.

I started both 2020 and 2021 positively; but I had a truly magnificently shitty time in between. Too little structure, too little confiding in people how shit I was feeling, too much time spent in front of the TV, too much wine, too little exercise, too much crap food and too little good food. But I thank my lucky stars that I am well and healthy, my children are well and healthy and, for the most part, my friends and family are well and healthy – with one notable gaping hole.

I started off 2020 with two living parents; I now only have one. My boys remember their grandad as lonely, depressed and unwell; but, most of all, they remember the fishing equipment he gave them for Christmas 2019 that he never got the chance to show them how to use. I saw my dad twice in the entire year before he died, and both times I didn't hug him or get any closer than two metres. As with the many many others who've been bereaved during this time, lockdown restrictions stole my last year with my dad and the last year that my boys could've had with their grandad. I think it's going to take a long time for me – and everyone else who's in the same position – to come to terms with that.

With this in mind, I may not have done much in the way of home schooling but I won't apologise for it. My boys are happy; they've been aware of the significance and severity of COVID-19 and we've spoken about it openly and honestly. I've answered their questions and they know the virus will not go away, that it will become endemic and that people will, sadly, continue to die. This past year has had us facing death at a time where we've not been able to support each other in our grief and in the realisation of our own mortality. That has been a hard thing to do.

This past year has brought death into our lives in droves. I've known of people who've died from COVID-19, one of whom was a young woman in her 30's with her whole life to live but instead died alone in hospital after contracting COVID-19 inside its walls. Our mortality was brought home through the many non-COVID deaths of 2020/21; my dad, who died as a result of COPD and heart disease, is just one of them. An inspirational woman who I followed closely – Fi Munro – passed away from ovarian cancer aged just 34 in July 2020 (if you want to read something really inspirational, her book *'How Long Have I Got'* is incredibly positive despite her terminal diagnosis). I know three families who've each lost a parent and a child in the past year (only one of these six deaths was COVID related; one was suicide and another the result of an unintentional drug overdose; and the rest cancer). And recently another of a family friend who was just 60 who died from cancer. There are many more that I'm aware of (and not just through the grim daily COVID deaths reported in the media and in government briefings), but that's 10 people in one year that directly affected myself or people I know. I don't know if I've ever encountered that much death before (although I admit that losing three grandparents within the space of two months back in 2017 comes pretty close).

There's no denying that death has been everywhere. I don't – and never have – hid the reality of illness and death from my kids; it's part of life and this pandemic has brought it all the closer to all of us. It doesn't help that I live across the road from a funeral home and we've had to bear witness to the significantly increased activity for the past year, as my boys regularly report *that's another [body] bag going in the back fridge, mum!'*. It's even in my home where my dad's ashes will remain until we're able to give him an appropriate goodbye. How ridiculous a notion is that? It makes me laugh (a little inappropriately but I either have to laugh or cry and laughing seems easier right now) that I'm keeping him in a cupboard until the government say it's okay for us to finally get together and say goodbye. Every time I go into that cupboard I'm faced with the reality of mortality. But where else do I put his ashes and my grief until we can let him go? I'm not alone in this; how many people are out there with trapped grief from the past year? Will we *ever* be able to release that grief or will it be stifled forever because so much time has passed? Will I ever properly cry for my dad? Will I ever feel that he's really gone? And if I don't, how do I reconcile this with my conscience? How do I come to terms with this and forgive myself? Can any of us who've lost a loved one during this time?

What has the pandemic and lockdown taught me about my own mental health and well-being? Honestly, nothing I didn't already know. I've faced those black periods of despair in my life before and I know what I need to do to clamber and claw my way out of that shit pit. I know that my go-to coping mechanisms are not helpful as I shut myself off from the world and lose myself in the oblivion that is pinot grigio and the escapism of TV. The lack of physically going to work and getting my boys off to school in the morning was welcomed with open arms, but not in a good way. My days had no structure, no routine. I hardly went outdoors, unless it was to buy food, and shutting myself off from the world was okay because the government told me so. And I suffered. I suffered from all of that, but most of all I suffered from loneliness and isolation. I can take a lot of emotional stress and pressure but that was one step too far. The lack of social contact almost broke me. Almost, but not quite. And why was that? Because I decided that enough was enough. I wasn't going to live like that anymore; I had to put the winter of discontent behind me.

I knew what I had to do and I did it. I've struggled with my mental health enough to know that it's only when *you* make change that your well-being will improve. I sat there for nigh on nine months in utter misery until I finally implemented the change that I knew would make a difference. Why did I wait so long? I wasn't ready to put in the effort. What gave me the nudge? I think it was simply the cumulative effect; I was just sick and tired of feeling sick and tired. I was fed up of going to bed miserable and waking up miserable and day after day after day being the same as the one before and the one that was to come. And yes, I had no reason to go out, I still wasn't able to mix with others and I was stuck at home but that didn't mean I had to live a life of misery and mediocrity. The turning point came when I finally decided I'd had enough of simply existing. I could either languish as I had been doing or I could flourish. I wanted to flourish.

Kicking the wine habit kickstarted my enthusiasm for life and my motivation to get shit done. And it's amazing what happens when you achieve something; you start to feel good about yourself again. I started this book in September 2020 but it was hard work and, well, honestly, it interrupted my wine drinking and TV watching (and this was before Bridgerton even landed on Netflix!). It was only in January 2021 after giving myself a good talking to and a kick up the arse that I pulled my finger out and got on with actually writing the damn thing. So, I gave up my beloved pinot, got out the laptop and never looked back. Even losing my dad a week after deciding to have a break from booze didn't derail me. If anything, it hardened my resolve to use my voice to help others.

My dad was incredibly depressed before he died, and it breaks my heart thinking of him alone. I wish I could've eased his pain even just a fraction. I don't wish that on anybody and if anyone is reading this and feeling that way I want you to reach out to someone and tell them exactly how you feel. I promise you the people who care about you will listen. My dad never shared how bad he was feeling, even though we could see it; he wasn't a big talker at the best of times. I had one lovely normal father-daughter phone call with him in October 2020 before things got too bad; one snippet of a moment to hold on to.

For those of you who don't have anyone to confide in; sometimes strangers are the best listeners. They're objective and sometimes it's just nice to hear those magic words *'it's okay to feel like that, your feelings are entirely valid and what you're going through is really shit'*. That validation can make all the difference. Because as I've already said, life isn't all sunshine, rainbows and roses; it's full of thunderstorms and huge big fucking thorns too, and the reality is that there really isn't much that any of us can do about that. So, we have to learn to roll with the punches, identify better ways of coping, take steps to improve our resilience and focus on the things that we *do* have. Change doesn't happen overnight, but with small steps and perseverance it *will* happen.

Will I stay off the booze for good? Probably not (although I need to shift the 'COVID 15' weight gain first!). But I will avoid using it as an emotional crutch as so many of those who contributed to the *'Life in Lockdown Duology'* admit to doing. We're human and we're flawed and that's okay. There is so much strength and power in admitting your flaws, folks.

An old school friend of mine had a really shit time of it during 2020. She's struggled with her mental health and addiction since our school days. I vividly remember her Insta stories one day as she bravely sat there, no make-up on, crying in her pyjamas and saying *'Hi, my name is [name], and I'm an alcoholic'*. My heart burst with pride but I could see how broken she felt. She's now over six months sober. Her mental health is still not great – I'm afraid sobriety isn't the magic pill to resolve *all* our issues – but it's a huge leap in the right direction. She shared her whole journey on Instagram and the response she got was phenomenal. Anyone who can give up their vice when they're in that shit pit deserve nothing but praise. They are not weak because they have a problem, they are strong because they have a problem and chose to overcome it. She rocks. If she can do it, anyone can.

I know I'm resilient but I also know how hard it is when you're depressed to work on bolstering your resilience; because who the hell wants to look inwards when they feel so utterly crap? Because all you see is your flaws. It's very difficult not to ruminate and dwell on things when you're depressed because your self-esteem is somewhere down at your ankles. This is work you need to do when you're feeling psychologically well.

I spend a lot of time nurturing my friendships and I receive an abundance of love in return. My friends are my chosen family. Unlike my family though, they aren't duty bound to stick around. If you don't treat them with the care and love they deserve then you won't reap the rewards. So, nurture those relationships, put the effort in and try as hard as you can to be the best that you can be for those people who you have chosen and who have chosen you. The problem is, that when I'm feeling shit the last thing I want to do is nurture relationships, in fact, I'd rather not communicate at all. Now, pre-COVID I already knew that this was my default setting, it has happened to me before and I swore at the time that I would never ever hide the extent of my struggles from my friends and family again.

I'm not ashamed or embarrassed to admit that I've been borderline suicidal before; I've experienced passive suicidal ideation but never active (that is, I've thought about it but never put any kind of plan in place). I know what it's like to suffer. I've been there and I promised myself when I recovered from rock bottom that if it ever happened again I'd share how I felt. Lockdown comes along and what did I do? Shut myself away again. What a bloody moron, eh? I still struggle with sharing as I don't want to place the weight of my struggles on other people's shoulders. I'm always saying to others that they can be brutally honest with me but I don't afford them the same in return. This is something I resolve to get better at because I know it's bullshit; the people in my life have suffered way more as a result of my hiding my troubles than they would have if I'd confided in them. I suppose this book is the start of that. This is me laid bare before you all, in my own words and pretty much unedited (bar the typos).

But I'm here to say that I'm okay. Even when I'm closed off I know what to do to look after myself and I know that I can speak to any one of my friends or family if I need to. I also say this: I will sometimes say I'm doing shit but I don't need the people I love to *do* anything, I'm just saying it's shit because it really is just shit and life isn't always rosy. This is a normal reaction to the normal ups and downs of life (I say that mostly for my mum's benefit whose default is *'are you okay, I'm really worried about you'* if I even hint at feeling a bit low on social media!). I appreciate the concern from the people I love but we all need to acknowledge that sometimes life is pretty crap and sometimes there is really nothing we can do about it apart from draw on our positive coping strategies, try to be positive and ride the fucking wave to the shore.

A huge part of feeling good about yourself is in having a sense of purpose and being able to contribute – this 'giving back' that people talk of. It sounds a bit like something people say because they're supposed to or they think it's the right thing to say, but it's true. Contributing to something bigger than yourself makes you feel better about yourself *and* benefits others, it's a win-win. I normally do voluntary human rights work in a women's prison but it was put on hold during COVID-19. I get such a sense of fulfilment from the unpaid work I do because I can see the direct benefit for others who need my help. This book has given me a different way of contributing when I was unable to fulfil this need in the ways I normally would. Getting a new job during the pandemic has also given me a new sense of purpose, passion and drive at work. I'm working long hours and loving it because, again, I can see how it makes a difference to people's lives. These are things which excite and motivate me as there are so many more people out there worse off than me.

I won't lie, it's been really tough with the general malaise of the pandemic and lockdown coupled with losing my dad. But never once has my enthusiasm waned from getting this book done (except for when a good friend suggested another writing project and I wanted to get started on that yesterday…I suspect I may need to go to Author's Anonymous). There's nothing more empowering and motivating than helping others and it gives you something to get out of bed for.

I had no other reason to write this book other than because I wanted to. I had no other reason to finish this book other than I wanted to. Why? Because it gave me a mechanism through which I could contribute to either helping people suffering from poor mental health and/or contribute to the wider debate around mental health awareness and stigma. This book was simply an idea that I decided to make real. It was challenging. It was stressful. It was a lot of pressure.

This stress and pressure was something that I didn't *have* to live with; I had no publisher breathing down my neck, no expectation of payment (nor need for it as I have my day job for that), no targets or timescales to meet (apart from my own), no motivation other than it might help someone else. All of this was self-imposed. But you know what? It's made me feel like I am contributing to something bigger than myself. It's given me purpose. It's given me focus. And all of that has brought me satisfaction and excitement. None of this has come from anyone but myself, a tiny idea that grew arms and legs that I stubbornly refused to give up on. For those of you who don't feel that you have a purpose, or don't know how to contribute I say this: don't wait for it to find you, go out and find it for yourself and, if it doesn't exist yet, create it. Only you can make it happen.

What the pandemic and lockdown has really taught me is to change how I frame my thinking. When I find myself saying *'I have to [insert activity]'* I now consciously have to reframe, and instead make myself say *'I get to [insert activity]'*. It's a bit like my own personal approach to cognitive behavioural therapy. So, instead of *'I have to stay home'* I say *'I get to stay in my warm and comfortable home'*, or *'I have to home school the kids'* I say *'I get to teach the kids and spend time with them'* and when I say *'I have to work from home alone'* I say *'I get to work, earn money and pay the bills'*. Another shift in mindset I use is adding 'for now' to the end of sentences. For example, I might think *'I feel stressed'* and it becomes *'I feel stressed for now'*. *'I am unhappy'* becomes *'I am unhappy for now'*. Of even *'my life isn't what I want it to be'* becomes *'my life isn't what I want it to be for now'*. It's not complicated, but it is a conscious choice to reframe those thoughts we all have that have the power to bring us down. It's amazing the power of just this simple shift in thinking. Try it, you might be surprised how it alters your mood.

I've done this to some extent for many years, this conscious reframing of my thinking. When I wake up feeling utterly miserable with no enthusiasm or motivation for anything (beyond coffee and Netflix, that is) I've consciously (and with a fair bit of effort) said to myself: *'you have two choices here; you either let your mood dictate a miserable day, or you choose to ignore your miserable mood and have a better day'*. Guess what? Choose the latter and your day is infinitely better than the alternative (believe me, I've done both). It's not easy, it takes a lot of bloody practice, but eventually this shift in mindset becomes second nature and pulling yourself out of the negative thought patterns gets easier. Fuck the ruminating…choose life.

I know that my situation during COVID-19 has been better than many others – a lot of us have been lucky when a lot of others haven't. It's easier to reframe your thinking when your whole world isn't collapsing around you as it has for many people in 2020/21. But, what the stories in this book show is that a huge part of coping with adversity is in our ability to see the good in our lives, even when the outside world is turning to shit.

The times in my life where I've really battled with poor mental health have been the times where I've been a fish out of water and I haven't had a clue what's coming or what to do about it. If you don't know what's coming you can't mitigate against it. I think part of the way to combat this feeling of complete lack of control is to accept that you can't control everything and learn to go with the flow. There is something incredibly empowering about giving up control and just trusting that it will work out. I am a firm believer in 'the universe has your back' and 'you are exactly where you're meant to be' mantras. I suppose this is part of cultivating positivity and the whole law of attraction school of thought. I know it sounds a bit 'out there' to some people, but in my experience it's true. At really dark times in my life it's this belief and mindset that has seen me through with hope and faith that things will work out; and it hasn't failed me yet.

I always, always trust my gut; if it doesn't feel right I don't do it. When I was in my final year of my undergraduate degree I was signed off my work with stress (work stress I hasten to add, life as a call centre debt collector was not pleasant) and I was told by management that if I was too stressed I had to consider what was more important – paying my bills or my degree. I chose my degree. Now, I had bills to pay but I was so unhappy that on the day I returned to work after being off for a month I handed my notice in, I didn't even have another job to go to. I set about applying for jobs where I could use my degree. On my last day in the call centre I received a job offer. It was only a three-month student placement but it would pay the bills and give me a bit of experience. This placement was extended to six months and on my last day there I found out I'd been successful in applying for a permanent post elsewhere, on better money too (which, to be honest, wouldn't be hard as my student placement salary wouldn't even be taxable now it was so low!). It wasn't ideal as it was a fair commute into Edinburgh every day (anyone who's had to commute via the Forth Road Bridge will understand the struggle). Both of those moves required a lot of faith that things would just work out the way they were supposed to; and they did. It didn't happen on its own, it required effort and action on my part in actively looking for opportunities, applying and attending interviews, but if I'd never followed my gut and quit that soul-sucking call centre job I'd never have ended up where I am and in a career that I love, pays the bills and fulfils that sense of purpose and contribution we all so desperately need to stay mentally well and resilient. My life hasn't been easy, but things have worked out (with hope and lot of grit and determination). My faith that the universe had my back and I'd get to where I needed to be – whatever that looked like – when I needed to be there was what gave me the motivation to keep plodding on, one foot in front of the other.

This same thinking got me through 2020. Nothing materially changed in my circumstances in the 12 months between March 2020 and March 2021 except a new job and losing my dad (oh, and I mustn't forget the optimism of the vaccine and a semblance of 'normal' at the end of the tunnel). I had hope that things would get better but I knew, just as I had before, that hope alone wasn't enough and that I needed to take steps towards making it better. I focused on development opportunities at work and at home and I made lifestyle changes and here I am; happier, healthier and hopeful. It's what we tell our kids all the time – *you can achieve whatever you put your mind to if you work hard enough'*. It's true, but with belief comes action – you need to put in the work.

I miss meaningful contact with my family and friends and I will never ever take that for granted again. I will relish every hug, every in-person smile, every shared car journey, every time you just pop into someone's house on the off-chance they'll be in for a catch up, every unplanned sneaked coffee with a friend before I start work, every hallway or kitchen chat at work, those chats over the top of your computer in the office, every team meeting, even those one-to-one supervision and appraisal meetings with the boss. I will appreciate every single moment of togetherness; no matter how small. Togetherness elevates us, the collective energy lifting us even out of the shit pit of despair.

When I think about what I could have achieved during 2020 if I hadn't frittered my time away with wine and let myself fester in front of the TV I feel angry at myself. But then I think *'well, life's a lesson and this book may never have been if it wasn't for your gloomy mental state and your desire to help people avoid what you went through'*. So, maybe it was a good thing after all? Maybe it was one of those times in life where it was just shit and it's taught me something about myself and about life that I would never have realised otherwise? As I said, life isn't all sunshine and roses, maybe 2020 was sent to teach me all of this; maybe it was sent to teach you something too?

I doubt that it comes as a surprise to any of you that we are facing the most significant mental health, physical health, economic, social and environmental crises in generations. We have not all been affected by this pandemic and lockdown equally; far from it, in fact. This world is rife with inequality. COVID-19 has not only highlighted domestic and global inequality, it has widened it. To steal the words of Damian Barr, more of us are on super-yachts and even more of us have lost an oar (possibly even two and maybe also have a hole in their boat). The gap between the rich and the poor has grown. We're most definitely not all in the same boat and, unfortunately, for some the storm will continue for many years.

The stories in the pages of this book *'Life in Lockdown I – Coping, resilience & positivity'* hint at the inequality that is running rampant across the world. Mental health is so inextricably interlinked with inequality that it's impossible to separate the two. Individual and global inequality, unsustainable practices and policies which enable them have been rife for too long. If COVID-19 has taught us anything it's that if we're serious about sustainability – economic, social and environmental – then it's time we act. It is appropriate then, and somewhat inevitable, that the impact of COVID-19 on collective humanity is the focus of *'Life in Lockdown II – Equality, equity & sustainability'*.

COVID-19 could be our once in a lifetime opportunity to address the structural unfairness that exists at home and across the world. It could be our chance to rectify the wrongs of our generation and the generations that came before us to make the world a better place for our children, grandchildren and the generations still to come. Let's not just fix what we already do when it's clear that it doesn't work and hasn't for some time – we need to stop trying to stick a square peg in a round hole. Let's start again. Let's look at how we can do it better to make the world a better place for *everyone*. Just as COVID-19 could've been sent to teach us something about ourselves, maybe it was sent to teach us something, collectively, too?

*"Learn to accept discomfort and uncertainty.
It will eliminate most of your imagined suffering."*

-Neil Strauss-

ACKNOWLEDGEMENTS

There are a number of people I owe a lot to for getting me through 2020/21. To be honest I struggle with where to begin. I couldn't possibly start without acknowledging two people who really gave me the drive to keep putting one foot in front of the other during this crappy time – my amazing kids; who have been wholly neglected in my determination to write this book (not in an intervention-type way, but in a not-doing-all-those-extra-nice-things-together-type of way). At times I never thought I'd finish this as what I wanted to say grew arms and legs (hence book two!), but I wanted to show my boys what you can achieve and how you can contribute when you put your mind to it. And the rest of my family, well, where would I be without you? It's been a fucking shitter of a year. Thanks for putting up with me.

And my chosen family. I can't put into words how much I love you and I count my lucky stars for each of you – Craig, Tara, Jenni, Aynsley and Katrina. I'm also incredibly fortunate to have a wider circle of friends with whom I can confide in (i.e. moan to) – Karen, Susie, Bas (thanks for the cover design once again!), Caroline, Emma, John, Shona, Wendy and Maxine. Some of you I've been friends with for a long time, some fairly recently, but you all helped me through lockdown at one point or another and put up with my moaning, tears, incoherent ramblings and general lack of enthusiasm. The medals are on their way.

To Gillian, Cat (particularly Cat who edited and proofed this with aplomb and humour into the early hours), Sarah, Gwen, Stephen, Colette and Nicola. I couldn't have asked for a better bunch of folks to work with during such a rubbish time. Our weekly video team meetings (i.e. work mingled with giggles and gossip) really were a highlight of my week. I miss them. And Cat and Sarah, our Zoom coffee breaks (and nights 'out' until 1am) certainly broke up the monotony!

Finally, and most importantly, thank you to those who shared their stories in either of the *'Life in Lockdown'* books. I know for some of you it was not easy – either recalling bad times or because writing is outside your comfort zone. I hope you take satisfaction in seeing your words in these pages and that you take pride that they may help others. If nothing else, I hope you're glad that you've shared your story of a time that will be recalled in history. You're all shining stars and your stories have inspired me. Thank you.

LIFE IN LOCKDOWN II:
THE GOOD, THE BAD & THE UGLY

Equality, equity & sustainability

– lessons from a worldwide pandemic

-coming soon-

www.ingramcontent.com/pod-product-compliance
Lightning Source LLC
Chambersburg PA
CBHW070334280726

48658CB00020B/47